GRANDPA PIKE'S
NUMBER
TWO

GRANDPA PIKE'S
NUMBER
TWO

FLANKER PRESS LIMITED
ST. JOHN'S

Library and Archives Canada Cataloguing in Publication

Grandpa Pike, 1944-, author
　Grandpa Pike's number two.

Issued in print and electronic formats.
ISBN 978-1-77117-715-3 (softcover).--ISBN 978-1-77117-716-0
(EPUB).--ISBN 978-1-77117-717-7 (Kindle).--ISBN 978-1-77117-718-4
(PDF)

　1. Grandpa Pike, 1944- --Anecdotes.　2. Newfoundland and
Labrador--Biography--Anecdotes.　3. Anecdotes.　I. Title.
II. Title: Number two.

FC2161.8.G73 2019　　　　　　971.8　　　　　　C2018-906563-X
　　　　　　　　　　　　　　　　　　　　　　　C2018-906564-8

PRINTED IN CANADA

This paper has been certified to meet the environmental and social standards of the Forest Stewardship Council® (FSC®) and comes from responsibly managed forests, and verified recycled sources.

Cover design by Graham Blair

FLANKER PRESS LTD.
PO BOX 2522, STATION C
ST. JOHN'S, NL
CANADA

TELEPHONE: (709) 739-4477 FAX: (709) 739-4420 TOLL-FREE: 1-866-739-4420
WWW.FLANKERPRESS.COM

9 8 7 6 5 4 3 2 1

We acknowledge the [financial] support of the Government of Canada. *Nous reconnaissons l'appui [financier] du gouvernement du Canada*. We acknowledge the support of the Canada Council for the Arts, which last year invested $153 million to bring the arts to Canadians throughout the country. *Nous remercions le Conseil des arts du Canada de son soutien. L'an dernier, le Conseil a investi 153 millions de dollars pour mettre de l'art dans la vie des Canadiennes et des Canadiens de tout le pays.* We acknowledge the financial support of the Government of Newfoundland and Labrador, Department of Tourism, Culture and Recreation for our publishing activities.

CONTENTS

DEDICATION

SOMETIMES I REFER TO MY DAUGHTER, LAURIE SHANNON, by her nicknames, "Duke" or "The Duke." If you've read many of my previous stories, you will know why. I also refer to her often as my "onliest baby girl." Onliest? That's not even a word, you say. Well, it is.

Some sources define "onliest" as the emphatic form of only, others as the intensive form. I call it the superlative form. How can "only" have degrees, you ask? I discovered this word a half-century ago when I was hitchhiking in the southern USA.

My "ride," a good-looking young guy about my age, wanted to stop at a diner just outside town for a bite to eat before we took off for Houston. As we were sitting, girls in nearby booths peered over at this guy with movie-star good looks. Naturally I speculated on which one he would choose and which one with whom I'd have half a chance.

Soon, other young women who were coming in or going out of the restaurant stopped by to speak to him. It seemed like he knew every good-looking female in the town—and the best ones twice, if you get my meaning. So I said to him, "I bet you have a lot of girl-friends."

"No," he said, taking out his wallet to show me a picture, "this is Michelle, my onliest."

So . . . I asked him about onliest, as I'd never heard that word before. Here's how he explained it to me. "She's the only one for me. The only girl I have. The only one I want. The only one I love. The only one there could ever be."

That's why I call Laurie Shannon my onliest baby girl. I dedicate this book to her.

DLHBG—and she knows what that means.

CHAPTER 1

QUIRKS AND
QUARE HABITS

We all have quirks—mannerisms or figures of speech which have become part of who we are—how people remember us. All of us have some prejudices, although some of us term them as preferences. Wouldn't it be boring if we all talked, walked, dressed, and looked identical? I'd be sick of lookin' at ya, I know that, even though you'd all be perfect—just like me.

AWESOME AND THE SUPERLATIVES

SOUNDS LIKE A BAND, RIGHT? CLEARLY NOT A HUMBLE one, either. That's not what I'm talking about, though. When I was a kid, if you thought something was really good or you liked it, it was "neat." In Yarmouth, Nova Scotia, when I was a teenager, it was "some good." Then along came "cool," "groovy," and "far out." "Far out" became "far freaking out" or its more liberated cousin, "far f------ out."

My parents would have said "it's the cat's pyjamas" or "the cat's ass"—although I never understood how something you liked or anything good could be compared to a cat's ass. Name something good that ever came out of a cat's ass.

Later on in life "excellent" became popular, and then "totally" or "like, totally." I'm talking in the white culture here. There were many other slang expressions, in other cultures, for something really good— something which you liked.

For the last few years, the most popular synonym for "like" was "awesome" or "totally awesome." It is applied to everything—the mundane and the extraordinary. For example, a hairdo can be awesome, so can a piece of pie, or the fact that someone made merely a passing grade in something.

If it is totally awesome that someone qualified for the Olympics, what do you call it when they win the gold medal? We need a new word.

These words are grossly overused to the point where absolutely anything can be "awesome," i.e. can fill you with awe, cause one to be filled with wonder and reverence. We should show more respect for our language.

I urge caution in using "awesome" so that, if something really extraordinary happens in your life, you won't be speechless for want of words to describe it.

Take the very word "caution" (which I urged). That is a word you see on warning signs in factories, in the instruction manuals for power tools, etc. I learned a new definition of that word when I was a young man, and I have never been able to get the image out of my head. See how it works with yours.

I used to do some work for an old farmer who lived up the road from us. He used that word regularly. If something was unusual or worrisome, he'd stand back and say, "Well, ain't that a caution!" I guessed that he meant it was something worthy of further study, or something to which one should pay close attention. I asked him, one day, what he meant. He stared at me for a few seconds like I was totally stunned, and then he explained.

"It's easiest if I give you an example. Let's say you are in my barn, working in a stall behind a horse, like you are now, and you see his tail go up. If you stay there, by and by you'll see his ass pucker. Get out of there right away. A caution is any movement in that outside ring of the horse's ass."

COMB-OVERS

THE *MERRIAM-WEBSTER'S DICTIONARY* DEFINES A COMB-over as "an arrangement of hair on a balding man in which the hair from the side of the head is combed over the bald spot."

That, I believe, is an inaccurate or at least incomplete definition. I've seen them combed from both sides, to meet on top. I've seen comb-overs combed from the back to the front—one in particular that I remember was so long he had it flipped back over at the front! How he kept it laying flat was a great mystery, and you don't ask the owner to explain. He has a secret—at least he thinks so. He's not likely to reveal his deception.

Somewhere there's a man with bushy eyebrows who is considering growing them out and combing them back over his bald head. Wait a minute—wasn't that what Leonid Brezhnev, the Soviet leader, did when he went bald?

I'm not picking on guys who dye their hair or buy "rugs" that look like dead squirrels. To each his own. I'm just talking about those marvels of engineering, comb-overs, that you sometimes see—mostly on windy days.

Some comb-overs are acceptable. I'm not entirely innocent. I have an acceptable comb-over. If you've always combed your hair straight back and you have only a small bald spot on top which is hidden by hair combed back in the normal way—is that wrong? What am I supposed to do? I should comb the hair away from the bald spot to highlight it?

Recently I was parked in front of a Home Hardware store, drinking my coffee, when an older man got out of his vehicle near me. He was wearing a ball cap.

As he turned to approach the store, the wind took his hat—and then went after his hair. The hair had been plastered flat across his head, and it suddenly flipped sideways, standing out about a foot and a half from his head. Slowly he manoeuvred himself around until the hair flopped back to where it was before. In an awkward sideways walk, with his head sitting about ninety degrees to his body, he moved toward where his hat had landed. As he bent to pick it up, the wind changed.

The green hat blew away and down to the end of the parking lot. He stared at it for a moment and then hollered: "To hell with you, I never liked Kent's anyway!" With that he proceeded toward the door holding his head at the right angle to keep his comb-over flat.

I don't know what the poor old gentleman was going in to buy, but if the staff saw the show and knew him, I hope they greeted him at the door with a free, brand new Home Hardware cap. Homeowners helping comb-overs. Proper thing, whaa?

FACEBOOK FRIENDS

FIRST OF ALL, ARE THEY REALLY FRIENDS? MOST OF US, IF we were to be brutally honest, could go down through our lists and eliminate the majority of our contacts and never lose a friend. Most are mere acquaintances. Some we have never met. Few could we message if we were down to our last dollar and needed rent money. Those few are our real friends.

We use Facebook for a myriad of reasons, some of which are: to promote our views, causes, or businesses, to keep up with gossip, to exchange recipes, to brag about our vacations, to share pictures of cute animals doing impossible things, or for posting philosophical "warm and fuzzies" written by others about concepts we don't even understand. Why? Because everyone else is doing it.

Some of us are not working, and we use it to pass the time— to stave off terminal boredom. No matter what you post, someone will "like" it, and it gives us, or our views, a little bit of validation. I spend too much time on Facebook. I am interested in the views of others. Unless they are true friends, though, I am not interested in seeing pictures of their babies, their trip to Paris, or what they are about to eat.

This little rant is probably going to make me some enemies. Someone will now "unfriend" me, so I'd better cut this short and find something else to do. Maybe I'll go on Facebook for a while. Oh, look at this picture of a cute little puppy dog and a kitten snuggling on the sofa! I better hit "like" on that. What's not to like? That's just precious, so it is.

Getting *Back* in Shape

I HAVE TO LAUGH WHEN I OVERHEAR A GROUP OF GUYS talking about getting back in shape. Usually they are eating in a fast food restaurant or drinking beer when the subject comes up. You know who gets back in shape? The guy who isn't there. He's quit talking about it and is doing it. He's too busy working, or working out, to hang around with these guys.

They'll bump into him a few weeks later and ask why they haven't seen him. They'll notice he's lost weight. He'll say he got tired of fast food, or the booze was bothering his stomach and he's laid off it for a while. The other guys will keep talking about getting back in shape and get no further.

After New Year's I saw many people out walking—every day—but now that number has dwindled. You see them out on a sunny day but not in any adverse weather. Most of them will drop out before Easter. Then a new crowd will start dieting and walking to get back in shape for the shorts and T-shirt weather.

I have no intention of getting back in shape, quite simply because I never was. Truth be told, neither were most of those who talk about doing it. I've never been to a gym and never ran or walked regularly. I lose weight during the summer if I have lots of physical work to do outside. I can lose it in the winter only by starving myself.

All that's gonna change. My mind's made up! I'm gonna get back in shape like everyone else. I'm going for a run now, the once—in my car—down to the Tim Hortons. I'm going to have a coffee with real cream and sugar, and a couple or three Boston cream doughnuts.

I intend to do that religiously for about three weeks. Why? If you are going to overcome an obstacle, you need to take a good run at it. I want to start farther back from the finish line. That way I'll have more to celebrate as the new slimmer, healthier, back in shape me! Would I lie?

I Wouldn't Change a Thing

EVERY TIME I HEAR SOMEONE SAY, "IF I HAD MY LIFE TO live over, I wouldn't change a thing," it makes me smile. Have they never made a mistake, or had anything bad happen which they could have prevented? I would change lots of things.

I'd spend more time studying history, science, and societal issues. I would spend less time in church and more time with music, art, and literature. I would get a degree in something instead of taking random individual university courses and then dropping out to go to work— so I'd have more money to spend chasing girls.

I would read even more than I have done and would have started questioning everything I was told at a much younger age. I would have gotten into a career other than business—something where *people* came first, not return on investment (ROI) and shareholder value.

I have seen too many people's lives ruined, careers ended, houses and cars forfeited to the bank because of greed in business. In the sector where I worked, rapid consolidation occurred with manufacturers, distributors, and retailers. One company bought another as a means of buying market share instead of earning it.

As soon as the consolidation was done, often the most knowledgeable, the hardest-working, and the most dedicated of the acquired employees were dumped upon the scrap heap. Many lost everything.

The new, larger company then lumbered along trying to combine two cultures without the leaders to make it happen.

I would move less—chasing job promotions and the ends of rainbows which one can never catch. As a result of all the moves, I really don't have a hometown. I missed a lot of school concerts and other events for my daughter. I missed being able to join any organizations that held their meetings through the week, as I was away travelling on business. I lost connections with old friends in communities where I had previously lived.

Those are some of the bigger changes I would make. I'd make a lot of other changes, too. I would not have started smoking. I would have tried to be more accepting of other people's beliefs. I would have tried to be more considerate of other people's feelings.

Anyone who says they would change nothing is either delusional, has never made a mistake, or as a result of being perfect has lived a charmed life. I haven't met the latter person yet. I'd make a lot of changes, so I would.

For example: I would have shown up for my second date with the nice girl who liked me—rather than going out that night with a new girl, a prettier girl. The one who liked me had few friends at school. She was a little overweight and self-conscious.

Her parents were so happy that she was seeing someone "decent." That evening she was to make supper for the four of us before we went out to a movie. How embarrassed she must have been when I didn't show up and didn't even call. She deserved someone way more decent than me—I hope she found him.

Premature Aging

ITIS THE DREAM OF MOST OF US TO LIVE LONG, BE HEALTHY to the last, and then with everything we wanted to do done, and our affairs in order, die quietly without pain, in our sleep. Few will be that lucky. Most of us will have some warning, even if only a few moments. Some will suffer long and welcome the relief when it comes.

I remember a visit to my mother, when she was older. I think we were going out to a restaurant for lunch. She had been dressed and ready for some time but was seated when I arrived. As she got up slowly from her chair, she groaned and sighed and said, "Don't ever get old, son. It's no good."

I didn't say anything to her, but I raised my eyebrows, thinking that perhaps the alternative is much worse. Is that what she wished for me? I knew she didn't, and she laughed when she realized what she had said, and said no more.

She's gone now, and I am about the same age she was when that incident occurred. I try not to complain about the new aches and pains, the health issues, the marginalization that I feel now that I am there.

Earlier in life, if I had aches and pains, a few days took them away. If I didn't feel good about a job or a place where I was living, I changed those things. With age the options narrow. Friends, as well as your career, go. Enemies, like aches and pains, and health issues, accumulate. Money goes out just as fast, but income flows in smaller volume.

"Living healthy" is the new mantra. If you don't, you will age prematurely, they say. Eat well, exercise regularly, and keep your mind occupied, and you will live longer.

I eat when I feel like eating, have no desire to exercise, so I don't, but I try to keep my mind occupied. My physically healthy friends seem to be dying just as quickly as the ones who ignore proper nutrition and exercise.

Frequently I hear of people out running or biking who drop dead of a heart attack. Their friends say, "At least she died doing what she loved." I bet if you could ask her if she'd rather be alive and reading a good book, eating chocolate, drinking wine, or having sex, she would have answered yes. When was the last time you heard of a man having a few cold beers on a hot summer day, in an air-conditioned tavern, keeling over dead?

So I'll do it my way. I am happy to be alive and coping with my inevitable decline. I hope that I can laugh and find some measure of humour or irony in everything I see and hear until that end comes.

All this talk about premature aging is just getting old—too fast.

The Keys to Paradise

IT SOUNDED LIKE THE TEN COMMANDMENTS, OR SOME other list of things that will get you to a special place in heaven.

I was travelling for a hardware distributor and was sent to fill in for another salesman, Bill, who had just left the company. We sold electrical, plumbing, builders hardware, paint, appliances, housewares, and a small assortment of giftwares—a total of perhaps 30,000 items in all. It was not unusual to be asked for something that you did not know that the company even carried.

So when the lady in charge of the houseware/giftware department in a large store asked me if we had any more of "the keys to paradise," I told her I would check it out and get back to her. I guessed that they were something like a set of oversized keys, probably plastic, with little Bible verses or mottos printed on them. Something that religious people would put up on the wall, next to a picture of Jesus, the Pope, or Joey Smallwood.

I wrote down her request (she wanted only one set) and then called the toll-free line to our order desk in Toronto.

The lady had gone on her break, so when our order desk guy asked me for a description, I had no answer. He didn't think we had anything by that name and suggested I call the old salesman and ask him. I called him and asked what they were. Bill basically dismissed me, saying he didn't know what I was talking about and he had to go now. I heard a woman ask him who he was talking to. He seemed real anxious to get off the phone.

When the old girl got back from her break with a fresh coat of makeup and lipstick on her tired, wrinkled old face, I told her that I had had no luck.

"I tried the order desk, and they didn't know what they were. Then I called Bill, and he said he didn't know, either."

"You didn't call Bill!"

"Yes. Why?"

"I hope he's not mad at me," she said, "but every time he came in here he would ask me out for a drink after work, or to have supper with him, or come over to his room later. I never went, but he'd always take his room keys out of his jacket pocket and say, 'Do you want the keys to paradise?'"

THE LIGHTER SIDE OF DEATH

THAT MAY SEEM A CONTRADICTION IN TERMS TO MOST people. Certainly there should be no reason for celebrating over the death of another. Death is an inevitable condition, however, and the billions of us who now live will face the same end. Why cry until it's time?

I've heard people say, "I'll probably have to work until I die." Well—I don't have to, but I want to work until the very last minute, if I can. As a matter of fact, I'd like to stay "active" afterward as well. I'll need co-operation from my family to be able to pull that off.

When I was younger, my teenaged daughter and I cooked up a revenge plot for a relative who shall be unnamed here. She looked down her nose at me because I smoked a pipe. We decided that when I die and they put me in the coffin with my arms folded, my fingers will be placed holding my favourite pipe.

The pipe will be empty of tobacco, but attached to the hidden mouthpiece of the pipe will be a long length of plastic tubing. The other end of the tubing will go out the window and down to the ground. My daughter will be holding that end and a lit cigarette. When the old girl is having her final look, and on a prearranged signal, Laurie Shannon will blow smoke through the tube and up into her face and eyes.

She'll get a start but probably try to look unfazed. She'd be thinking, "Look at that, the old heathen dead only these three days, and already he do be blowing his smoke up from the bowels of hell."

I spent most of my life around retail. Sometimes, late at night when I can't sleep and am contemplating my own mortality, I get crazy ideas for retail promotions.

A dead person could be used (with their prior approval, of course) to help sell products. Why? Because they can do anything a mannequin can do and look more realistic. Mind you, they couldn't do it for long—but what a way to pick up a few dollars to help defray the cost of the funeral!

How better to sell a bed, for example, than having an attractive person laying on it, "asleep?" Here's what the salesman might say:

"This bed's some comfortable, so it is. Buddy lay down on it and hasn't moved once. He's been there since we opened this morning. We have only one left, and the sale ends today! Don't he look comfortable, though? Hardly moving, luh, luh!"

Meanwhile, over at the funeral home, Bill, who's just coming on shift, is panicking. After doing a count, he finds a body missing!

"Anybody seen the McCavour cadaver?" he asks worriedly.

The other mortician tells him, "No problem, Bill, he's over at The Brick working a day shift, and he's doing a graveyard tonight—night watchman—over at the 'Toys B We.' He'll be back in the morning—in plenty of time for his funeral."

EXPLORERS—WHO WAS THE FIRST?

O N MAY 29, 1953, TWO MEN REACHED THE SUMMIT OF Mount Everest, the highest mountain peak on earth. One of those men was Edmund Hillary. One was not. Anyone remember his name? Hillary was knighted for his effort and became Sir Edmund Hillary. The other guy (Tenzing Norgay) got the George Medal and is now known to most as "the Sherpa guide." Ever hear of the George Medal? Neither did I.

Both men were awarded these honours by Great Britain. Hillary was thirty-four at the time of the climb and Norgay one year shy of forty. Hillary was a white New Zealander. Norgay was "a brownish kind of fellow, yes—but an awfully nice sort."

I don't know which one first put his footprint on the summit. I don't care. It was a team effort. The only two in the whole expedition who were well enough to go the last 300 feet were Sir Edmund Hillary and old Wassisname Norgay.

In 1492, Christopher Columbus (an Italian named Christoforo Columbo), who was known as Christóbal Colón in Spain, sailed west from Europe and "discovered" America. Nobody knew it was there before. Even the natives, who all spoke a strange foreign language, didn't know! Who knew? Well, the Europeans didn't know, for sure, even though Norsemen had made many trips and even lived there for a while—almost 500 years earlier. To be fair, though, Newfoundland was a good bit farther north of where Columbus landed.

Let's forget about the Vikings and pretend that Columbus discovered the New World—better known today as the Western Hemisphere. Do you think that Columbus himself was the first to step ashore?

I mean, these people had spears and torches and, who knew, maybe weapons you'd only find by doing a cavity search. He wasn't going to go ashore first to test the water, so to speak. Columbus likely had a few old Italian buddies travelling with him—even though he was working for Spain. I'll bet he sent them ashore first. Mario and Luigi, likely, were the first Europeans to set foot in South America!

Mario and Luigi waded ashore to meet the natives, and when they returned to the boat, Mario said, "They seem a-nice, even if they speak a-funny. They say you shoulda come to supper, Christo. Luigi, he make it a date with the chief's daughter, and she have two nice-a friends!"

That's probably how it happened, but does anyone remember Mario and Luigi? Of course not—why didn't they think of changing their names to good English ones like Columbus did—or like Ahmed, Hassan, Karam, and Muhammad did—those four Middle Eastern guys who followed Jesus (you know—Matthew, Mark, Luke, and John)?

Who was the first *astronaut* in outer space? That's easy. Yuri Gagarin of the USSR gained that distinction in 1961. But he wasn't the first. He was the first human. The first astronaut was a rhesus monkey named Albert II, who flew past the 100-kilometre boundary of space in 1949. The first known *life forms* in space were fruit flies—seriously—in 1947.

What I wanted to know when I heard about the fruit flies was—why? All they had to do was send along some fruit and it would have had fruit flies on it by the time they got back. It was, of course, in an effort to see if they could survive. They did. Many monkeys and other animals didn't, including Albert I. Aren't we just so nice to all the "lesser" creatures—human and otherwise—giving them the first crack at everything, if not the glory?

NICE DAY?

IT WAS A WARM, SUNNY DAY IN MAY WHEN I LEFT HALIFAX to fly to St. John's, Newfoundland. My first time back since I left as a child, I couldn't wait to get back to the land of my birth. Looking out the window of that EPA flight, the place looked barren and forbidding as we floated over rocks and snow and tundra and countless ice-covered ponds. As we got lower, flying into Torbay Airport, it didn't get any better.

The runway was free of snow but wet. A side wind kept nudging us toward the banks of melting snow to the right of us. I'm pretty sure they were snowbanks—the fog made it hard to tell. I walked with my seatmate toward the terminal, with the horizontal rain soaking one side of me, the wind threatening to blow the coat off my back.

As we neared the terminal on this near-freezing morning, my companion—a Newfoundlander—turned to me and said with a smile and not a hint of sarcasm, "Nice day!"

I laughed, as a bit of comic relief can sometimes ease an unpleasant experience. He looked at me kind of funny, and we parted inside the terminal as he went to pick up his luggage. With only a carry-on, I proceeded out through the front door of the airport to the taxi stand. The driver held the door, and as I was getting in, his first words were, "Nice day."

This time I just nodded and smiled. No point in picking a fight with a guy who looks like he may be out only on temporary day parole.

And so it went. Almost everyone I met that day remarked how nice a day it was. I'm thinking, *How bad must it be, normally, if this is a nice day? What am I in for when the weather decides to turn foul?* I soon found out. It snowed, it blew, it dropped those stinging little ice pellets, but the horizontal rain was the clincher. Rain is supposed to come *down*, not at you sideways, like a snake.

One evening, later that week, I checked into a small motel, out around the bay, cold and wet and hungry. They had no dining room, but they did have a bar where they served fries and hamburgers. I sat at the bar and had a couple beers to warm up. I got talking with a friendly old local guy who was one of the first that week to not greet me with "Nice day."

I bought him a beer and decided to ask him about that expression. "On the mainland we only say that if it is warm, sunny, and not too windy," I told him. "Does it mean something else here, or are these really nice days compared with what you usually get?"

A little bit of both, according to him. Apparently nobody comes to Newfoundland for the climate, but there's a folklore aspect as well. Old sailors believed that Neptune or the sea gods controlled the weather. If you complained about the weather, they would get even with you next time you sailed. From that belief came an old expression: "Praise the weather when ashore." Now it was starting to make some sense.

Over the years I've run into every conceivable type of weather in Newfoundland, sometimes all in the same day! A few years ago, a friend of mine who runs a tourist boat here went to California for a vacation. While it's untrue that it never rains in California, where he landed it is sunny ninety-five per cent of the time along with ninety degrees Fahrenheit.

He told me, "I said 'nice day' to the guy at the car rental counter, and he looked at me as if to say, 'What did you expect?' He got friendly after a while, and he wondered what I do in Newfoundland. I told him about my iceberg and whale-watching tours, and he was really interested. I gave him my card. He phoned me this week, and he's coming up this spring for a trip."

When that Californian got off the plane at St. John's Airport in Torbay, in weather you wouldn't let your dog out in, and everyone says "nice day," I hope he was polite and wise enough to agree before he stepped aboard buddy's boat.

— CHAPTER 2 —

PEOPLE I WON'T FORGET

It is said that friends come and go. I believe that could be more accurately termed as acquaintances come and go. True friends do not desert you. They leave you only when one of you dies. Then there are those people who you never got to know well—never became close friends with—but still they left a lasting impression. Others became lifelong friends. Some have died, but I will always remember them. These are a few of my favourites.

Joey—Yes, *That* Joey

I HEARD A LOT ABOUT HIM WHILE I WAS GROWING UP. MY father was a big fan. They knew each other in Newfoundland before we moved to Canada in 1948. I always wanted to meet him. When I was travelling on business in Newfoundland in the late 1970s, I decided to try.

At the time Mr. Smallwood was working on his massive final literary work, the *Encyclopedia of Newfoundland and Labrador*. It was early September, and my father's birthday was coming up. I thought I would go out and buy a book and somehow try to get Joey to autograph it as a gift to my father.

I was at my girlfriend's house in Placentia, and somebody said, "Why don't you just phone him?" Sure enough, he was in the phone book, and when I got up enough nerve, I dialled his number. "Joey Himself," as some of his detractors used to call him, answered.

"Sure," he told me, "I'd be delighted to autograph *and* inscribe a book for your father." *Wow*, I was thinking, *I am about to meet the only living Father of Confederation!* I asked where I might find one of his earlier books.

"You should be able to find them in any bookstore in the city," he told me, "but why not come over to my office tomorrow? We have a good selection there." He told me about his office on Portugal Cove

Road, gave me directions, and even told me at which intersections I should be careful. He said that any time during the day would be fine. I went to town early and made a couple of sales calls, but I waited until late morning before I went to see Joey.

Just inside the door of a huge room sat a middle-aged lady—receptionist or secretary to Joey, I presume. The room was buzzing with activity as editors, writers, and others were milling about, and at desks, and on typewriters, and pasting up pages, and on the phones gathering information. I told the lady why I was there.

She pointed to a small, older, white-haired gentleman at a desk near the back of the room. "He's right over there," she said. He had a phone to his ear. Noticing my hesitation to move, she said with a smile, "Go on over, he'll talk to you." As I approached his desk, he was still in conversation, so I stood back until he was done.

"I just need to know," he was saying to the person on the other end, "is a quintal a measure of weight or volume?" He got his answer, wrote something down, and ended the call. Then he saw me, and he rose, almost jumping to his feet. I introduced myself, and we shook hands.

"Pike," he said, "that's a good Newfoundland name." Then he started telling me about my family. He went back several generations. Next he told me that at one time he knew every man woman and child in Newfoundland. He remembered my father, "a small man, like myself—a salesman when I knew him. How is Rod?

"The surname Pike goes back a long way here," he said. Then he proceeded to tell me the story of the Irish princess Sheila NaGeira, and the English pirate Gilbert Pike, who settled in what is now Carbonear and had the first non-native child born in North America. "That story will be in my encyclopedia," he added.

"Would you like to have a look around?" We walked around, and he showed me plaques and citations and photos on the walls—of kings, queens, dictators, celebrities, and politicians with the little guy in the horned-rimmed glasses and bow tie. He took his time and answered my questions.

I was thinking, *Here is a man at an age where many are on the deck in a rocking chair, if not already dead, and in this room he is documenting everything he knows and can compile about the province in this huge undertaking—a Herculean task even for a young man—and yet he has all the time in the world to talk to me.*

I chose a book. He autographed and inscribed it and told me to give his best wishes to my father. I was walking on air. I shook his hand goodbye, walked out the front door, and was halfway to my car before I realized that I hadn't paid for the book!

Hurrying back in, I apologized profusely to the receptionist, who smiled and said as she took my money, "He has a way of doing that to people."

I glanced back toward his desk before I went out the door, but his head was down and he was buried in his labour of love once more. I never got to see Joey again.

THE WIFE LIKES YOU

THE FIRST TIME I EVER HEARD THIS EXPRESSION WAS in Cape Breton in the early 1970s. J.W. Stephens Ltd., a building supply business located in Sydney, Nova Scotia, was a large account for my company. Bill Stephens was the owner at the time, and you needed to involve him in every transaction. He wanted all salespeople to make appointments as well. Somehow I got away without doing so. When you are travelling a huge territory, living in hotels, and doing sixteen-hour days, it is just impossible to pinpoint exactly when you will arrive.

Bill was a quirky kind of person—a gregarious guy, and a natty dresser. My very first call on him, he took one look at my sports coat—which in those days was some gaudy kind of thing—and jumped up out of his big swivel chair.

"What a great jacket! It looks about my size. Can I try it on?"

I let him, of course, like you would, and he went out of his office to a mirror to see how it looked. He wanted to know where he could get one like it. I gave him the name of the store in Ontario. He was so impressed with it that I offered to give it to him. He politely declined, but if liking my jacket was just a ruse to make sure I remembered him, it worked.

This story is not about Bill, however, but a young guy named Jim, who worked in the warehouse. Jim was really helpful in telling me what products were low in stock and what kinds of deals the competitors were offering. He also took lists up to Bill for me and came back with purchase orders. One day, perhaps the hottest day of that summer, I was at the store and went to see Jim out in the warehouse.

It was so hot out there it would make you dizzy. Jim's T-shirt was soaked with perspiration and his face wet.

"Jim," I said, "how do you suppose an ice-cold beer would taste right now?"

"My Blessed Virgin," he said, "I'd do a dozen after work, but payday's not till Friday."

"Okay," says I, "then after work it is, and I'm buying."

I had to make another call, and I got back to pick up Jim at closing. His wife was working at the hospital and had their car. I asked him where he wanted to go. He apologized for being broke but said if I could afford a six-pack, we could pick it up at the "controllers" and go to his place to drink it. That way we could get something to eat, too.

It sounded good to me, so off we went. He smiled like a child on Christmas morning when he saw me coming out of the liquor commission with a box of twenty-four—his brand. When we got to Jim's, we put some in the freezer to cool and drank a warm one. We kept feeding the freezer, but we drank the first few faster than the freezer could cool. Finally, after about five each, we had our timing down. It was hot in Jim's house—even with the windows open—not a breath of air. I've never enjoyed a cold beer as much as I did that day.

At about seven thirty or so, Jim's wife pulled in the driveway. We still hadn't eaten and were feeling no pain. I thought we were really in trouble. I started putting the empties in the case and trying to look serious, like we'd been doing business. She was pleasant, friendly, and not upset at all. I made a few jokes and complimented her on the decor—pouring on a little bit of charm, which I thought might help

Jim later. Then I had to go to the bathroom because, as you know, you don't buy beer—you only rent it.

I figured I'd get a taxi back to the hotel and Jim could bring my car back in the morning. No point in wearing out his wife's patience. But when I got back, they were both at the table sipping on a cold one, arms around each other. I suggested that it was probably time for me to move on.

"Oh no, b'y," said Jim, he and his wife both smiling at me, "have another one, sure. The wife likes you."

A Portrait of Human Weakness

1971—IT WAS A YEAR WHEN MANY WONDERFUL AND TER-
rible things happened. The Charles Manson trial, the *Apollo 14* and
15 moon landings, the awarding of compensation to the families of
the Kent State University protest victims (four dead in O-hi-o). Over
13,000 Vietnam War protesters were arrested in three days on Nixon's
orders. George Harrison released "My Sweet Lord," and John Lennon's
"Imagine" and Don McLean's eleven-minute "American Pie" hit the
airwaves. It was just a couple of years after the Summer of Love and
Woodstock, and the last year my best friend, Peter, and I hitchhiked
from Burlington, Ontario, Canada, to Mexico.

We were in Baton Rouge, bullfrog fishing with a couple of Cajun
guys, and the next morning backtracked to Mobile, Alabama. I insisted we go there because of Dylan's song "Stuck Inside of Mobile
with the Memphis Blues Again." Peter would agree only if we would
go through Oklahoma on the way back from Mexico. He wanted a
picture, standing under the WELCOME TO MUSKOGEE sign, smoking a
marijuana joint. I still have that picture.

When we got back from Mobile, we spent a couple days in the
French Quarter in New Orleans. We listened to music, drank beer,
and most of all sought out female company—like you would. On the
second day, I met an attractive young street artist drawing portraits for

tourists on Bourbon Street. I chatted with her while Peter went into a bar to get us a couple beers. She thought I had an interesting face and wanted to do a picture.

I told her that we were leaving the next morning on our way to Mexico, but if time had permitted I would have loved to get an oil portrait done.

She said that she could do a couple of sketches and try—but she would prefer to have me sit for her. Unfortunately, she didn't have time that day to get started—and tomorrow we'd be gone.

As we were talking, a tourist with a Polaroid camera hung around his neck walked by.

"Sir," she asked him, "would you take a picture of my friend for me? He's going away tomorrow." The gentleman was only too happy to oblige, and after waiting a minute for it to develop, he handed it to her.

"I can do it from this!" she told me. We agreed on a price, I gave her my address and a $20 deposit, and as other tourists were starting to crowd around looking at her pictures, we moved along. I didn't know if I'd hear from her again. I didn't for some time, but when I received a parcel from New Orleans in February 1972, I knew instantly what it was.

It was a very well-executed oil on canvas, with the original Polaroid picture attached. With only the one pose, and poor colouring in the Polaroid picture, she did me proud. I have forgotten the full price that we agreed on, but it was probably around $50. I never paid her the balance—and of that, truly, I am ashamed.

There are no worthy excuses— nevertheless, here are mine. I put it off for a few weeks until I could spare the money. Then I got transferred to another store and had to move and buy some furniture. Then I decided to wait until I got my tax refund. By now I had the painting packed in a box and didn't take it out for years and completely forgot about it.

When I unpacked it I thought perhaps her address or even her surname may have changed because she was a young single girl when I met her.

I tried long-distance information, and they had no one by that name in New Orleans. I thought about putting an ad in the newspaper there to see if I could locate her. I never got to it. There were no social media or Google or even computers then to aid the search.

I was making less than $100 a week before deductions at the time. I didn't have a lot of money to spare. I reasoned that it wasn't worth it to spend as much as I owed her on an ad to find her. (I'll bet that she would likely have disagreed.) Then one day, recently, I was Googling "New Orleans Jazz," and I came to a newspaper article about New Orleans jazz art paintings by an artist named Ann deLorge. She lived in Georgia, and I found her website! I was sure it was her. I had been searching for Ann *DeLonge*—as that's how her signature on the painting appeared.

In 1971, the $20 or $30 I owed her would have bought a lot of groceries or paid her rent for a couple of weeks. It was very wrong to have let this slide for so long. With inflation, that could be worth over $300 now. I saw on her website that she still did portraits, and she listed her prices by size.

I was going to send her the amount I thought I owe her—with inflation. I believed that was only fair, because if she were doing it now—16 x 20—it would cost me $720, according to her website. Today I couldn't afford it. I'd send her a letter of apology, a copy of the photo, and a picture of the portrait—as she may have forgotten about me.

I had no idea, of course, how badly Ann may have needed her money at the time.

I hoped Ann didn't go hungry or fail to meet her rent one week, so long ago, when we were young and I was so inconsiderate. I hoped she could find it in her heart to forgive me. I hoped she didn't hate me, but I wouldn't have blamed her if she did.

I didn't write the letter as I intended. I sent the story, as above, instead. I enclosed a copy of the original Polaroid, a picture of the painting, and a bank draft. I heard back from her by mail shortly thereafter.

The first few words of Ann's response, "My Dearest Laurie," let me know where she was going with her reply. It was a good place. She had forgotten about me. How many would have carried a grudge all those years? Ann forgave me, and she was so pleased to get the "story." One can't always go back and fix his stupid mistakes, for a number of reasons. It's good to fix the ones you can, though. I feel better now. Thanks, Ann.

Running Away to a Better Place?

SHE BURST OUT THROUGH THE FRONT DOOR OF THE apartment building, a young child on her hip, a purse on her arm, and a suitcase in her other hand. A couple of garments protruded through the seams of the hastily packed bag. She was a woman in a hurry to get gone.

I was parked at the curb, behind the wheel with the phone to my ear—on a conference call. She paused, glanced at me like she was wondering if she knew me, then turned away and hurried up the sidewalk. There was no traffic, the call was boring (my only participation was listening) and seemed to go on forever but in reality was only about five minutes.

As she turned the corner at the first intersection, I lost sight of her. Bored with my phone call, I started speculating on her story. I guessed her husband had just left for work or to go out drinking. After enough years of putting up with him, she decided to walk out. She had the baby, the baby's things, and a change of clothes, and she wanted to put as much distance between her and the abusive husband as possible before he got back.

When I got off the call, I proceeded up the street and turned in the direction the young lady had gone. Not to follow her, but because it was the main route which I had to travel to get to the airport. There was little traffic at this time. I saw her walking, and when she heard my car coming, she stopped, set down the small suitcase, and stuck up her thumb. I *never* pick up hitchhikers. It's just too dangerous.

But the lady looked in distress and had a small child. I pulled over. She put her suitcase in the back and got in the front with me.

"Are you going near the airport?"

"You're in luck," I told her. "That's exactly where I'm going."

"Thanks so much," she said. "We overslept, and I have to get there."

We drove along in silence for a few minutes. I figured if she wanted to talk she would start the conversation. She was probably going away somewhere safe, perhaps to her parents' place—somewhere away from the abuse she could no longer take. She kept glancing at her watch and looking worried. So, finally, I said, "Afraid you are going to miss your flight?"

"Miss?" she asked. "No, I'm meeting my husband's flight. He's been in Afghanistan. This is his first time home since our baby was born. Everything's all right now, though. Thanks to you, Sarah will get to meet her father when he arrives."

I couldn't make sense of her suitcase, though, so I had to ask.

"Not to pry, but why the suitcase?"

"We are staying at a hotel tonight," she said. "I only wish we had a babysitter," she continued with a slight blush. "Wanted to have a nice dinner, a couple drinks, and get to know each other again."

The rest of the way to the airport she told me about her husband, Jim. She loved him, that was for sure. I didn't know why she was so open with me; perhaps because I was an older man with grey hair—like a grandfather. She had known him since grade school. He brought a single rose from his mother's garden to school for her thirteenth birthday.

They kissed when she was fourteen. She had kissed no other man since. They were sweethearts through high school. All he ever wanted to do was be a soldier. After cadets, and an eye surgery which corrected his vision, he joined the reserve and then went to college to become a schoolteacher. Finally, he got called to active duty and took leave from his teaching job.

He was a high school gym teacher and she a nurse—off work since the baby came. Not enough time in to get maternity leave. Money was tight. She had been worried about him every minute he had been gone. She couldn't sleep at night. Having the baby helped during the day, and he wrote her twice a week. He'd been injured. Nothing serious, but they were sending him home for a while. He was her hero. She wouldn't want to live without him.

I had lots of time until my flight, and her husband's was still ten minutes out, so I walked with her to Arrivals, carrying her suitcase, and waited with her. When he finally came around the corner, I recognized him from her description. He was tall, handsome, in full uniform but walking on crutches—and missing one leg from the knee down. She hadn't said a word about that! She hadn't said he was coming home for good.

I backed off a little as they reunited, and a few seconds later a buddy of his, also in uniform, came along and got Jim's luggage together on a cart. He would take them in his car to the nearby hotel. As I watched the young couple, I couldn't help but think that while there was more of him that went away than that which came home, he still came home a bigger man. He was a father now and a hero to at least two people.

I wished them well and left for Departures to catch my flight. I kept thinking about how we jump to conclusions and how very wrong we can get things.

I hoped his buddy took a room down the hall and looked after the baby for a while that evening. I s'pose he did, because that's what good friends do.

I also hoped that the school board would be inspired enough to see the benefit in hiring a one-legged hero to be their gym teacher. All heroes—including the spouses who wait for their soldiers—deserve a helping hand, whether it's a little babysitting, a good job, or just a ride to the airport. They, too, are brave—those who wait behind. I'm quite sure of that conclusion.

STAN

I N 1975, I WAS WORKING WITH CREST HARDWARE AS ZONE
manager in eastern Ontario for their chain of hardware stores. Even
after being in Ontario for ten years, I still had a strong connection to
the east coast and decided to move home. That's when I met Stan.

He interviewed and hired me for a position in the Maritimes with
Dominion Hardware. At the time Stan was in his early forties, and I
was a few months shy of thirty. A big guy with hands the size of catchers' mitts, a great dry sense of humour, and a full head of completely
grey hair, I took to him right away. He was a kind of mentor or even
a father figure to me, despite the fact that we weren't all that far apart
in age.

Stan was wonderful in sales meetings. I listened to every word.
You never knew when he would use a throwaway line or irony to get a
point across. At one sales meeting just before our trade show, he called
us to order and started like this:

"First of all, I'd like to make an announcement. I understand that
the salesmen are having a beer-drinking contest tonight. No harm
in that. Have fun. Just remember that we have serious business first
thing in the morning. Apparently there are teams for tonight's contest:
Southern Ontario, Northern Ontario, The Maritimes, Newfoundland,
etc.

"Since we have only one employee in Newfoundland, young Peter has recruited a couple of very capable dealers to his team. I wish you all luck.

"If I was a betting man, however, I think I would pick the Newfoundland team. I understand they have been practising for three days now.

"I don't know what first prize is, but second prize is from me and goes to all who show up sober and ready to go to work in the morning. Did somebody ask what second prize is? You get to keep your job."

I watched Stan—how he dressed, how he conducted himself, and how he spoke. I copied everything I could. Like my earlier boss, Hank, in the food business a few years back, I had the greatest admiration for him.

When things started to get tougher in the hardware business in the early 1980s, with consolidation and more competing programs or banners for the dealer to choose from, Dominion Hardware felt the pinch. Stan was strong—constantly encouraging our owners to make positive changes and to modernize. I'm sure he kept dozens of dealers onside, who would have otherwise left, by the sheer strength of his resolve, personality, and vision.

I had a terrible disagreement with Stan over a contract one year. We reached an impasse, and I resigned from the company and went with a competitor. Stan was right, and so was I. Doctor Dingwell and others worked behind the scenes to get us back together. It happened, and I went back to work with them. Stan and I had a private meeting. We agreed to bury the hatchet and never to speak of the matter again. Neither of us ever did.

Later, after my daughter was born, I thought I should come off the road and be home more. I bought a building supply yard and left full-time work with Dominion Hardware.

Stan kept me on, though. He hired me, part-time, for special projects—one day a week. The first project was to try to fix a store that wasn't performing well. I had a free hand, and we made the store work. After two years, though, my wife and I decided to sell our own store, and Stan hired me back full-time with the company.

When the Cochrane family sold Dominion Hardware, the new owner leaned heavily on Stan for guidance, advice, and for the day-to-day running of the company. Unfortunately, it was all in vain, as the handwriting was already on the wall. The company went into receivership in 1987, and Stan protected only two guys from the east to work with the receivers—Doctor Dingwell, to whom I reported, and me.

Within weeks the company was sold off, piecemeal, and we were all out of work. Stan went to work with a regional Ontario distributor. Dave went with Pro Hardware, and I went to Premdor. Later, when the company which Stan was with got sold, he attempted retirement. It didn't work out for him. He needed to work—not because of money but out of drive and habit.

Then Ace Hardware came to Canada, and Stan was hired for special projects such as doing presentations to new dealers and coordinating the remodelling of stores. He loved it. As they got established, he was used less and less, and finally he was gone around 2000.

I talked with him by phone quite a few times in the years after we no longer worked together, and I always heard some new funny lines from him and got wind of industry rumour or news of which I was unaware.

One year, after the annual ABSDA show, some Dominion Hardware alumni met at my place. We had a few drinks, phoned Stan, and sang him a song, "Dominion Hardware Blues," which I had written. Stan loved it.

I went to work for Ace Canada myself later—about a year after Stan was gone from the company. In 2003, I was in London, Ontario—after Ace Canada was sold to Sodisco-Howden. I called Stan, who lived there. We went out to dinner, and he lamented that not only was he not working but that after he was retired nobody phoned anymore.

He'd put fifty years of his life into the industry, ran a company, helped develop several franchise programs, and was a wealth of knowledge—but none of his old colleagues called him. I could only imagine how he felt. It had to be devastating.

One thing he mentioned was the Estwing Gold Hammer award, which is given for fifty years in the industry. He didn't get one. I went to work on this when I got home, and within a couple of months, thanks to Ken O'Meara of Estwing and Michael McLarney of *Hardlines* newsletter, he got his gold hammer and his dinner.

I haven't talked with him in a few years now. The last Christmas card I sent him was returned undelivered, and later I was told that he had developed a cognitive disorder. Doctor Dingwell told me that Stan passed away about two years ago.

I have just turned seventy-four, and despite a wealth of experience in recruiting dealers to banner programs, supervising chains of stores, and selling hardware and building materials, I too came off the road, unable to find a suitable job.

Like Stan, I am driven and want to work simply because I need to be busy, and I loved what I was doing. I rarely get an email or a call from an old colleague. Ten years ago I could only imagine how Stan felt. Now I know.

Too bad our society values youth over experience and knowledge. Too bad our perceived value declines a lot quicker than our real worth. As Stan would probably say, with a laugh, if it's about as long as it is tall, I guess that kind of makes it square, eh?

I can only add, no matter how far you travel or how high you climb, it still takes the exact same time to get back to square one—although it defies logic and the laws of physics. RIP—S. W. "Stan" Leitch.

CLEO

SHE WAS ALL MOVIE ACTORS AND MUSICALS, LITERATURE and live theatre, and art—dreaming and yearning with stars in her eyes and hope in her heart. She absolutely loved poetry. Her real name wasn't Cleo, but that's what she called herself. Dark-complexioned with coal-black hair, she wore heavy eyeliner, mascara, and brightly coloured stripes running horizontally from the outside corners of her eyes. This is how she believed Cleopatra would have looked.

She talked a mile a minute and excitedly about her hopes and dreams. She was bored by the mundane and anything else that didn't interest her. I listened to her more than talked with her. She was always happy, expected the best from people, and believed her dreams would come true. She was eighteen and I was a couple years into my twenties. Her passion extended to kissing but not beyond. I was fascinated by her—almost hypnotized.

We hung out together for a while, in the era of coffee houses, folk music, and hippies—before that term was popular. One day she was gone—just gone as though she had left town without time to say good-bye. I don't know if she lived with her parents and they moved, or if she simply hitchhiked out. She never said where she lived—just "in a house."

No one I knew ever saw her again. That was over fifty years ago. I have no idea where she went, why, or how she lived her adult life. I've often wondered if she was lucky enough to realize any of her dreams. I hope so. Here's a short poem for you, Cleo.

Cleo, Cleo, who are you?
Did your dreams like birds soar free?
Did you find your rhyme and reason?
Did you ever cry . . . like me?

CHARLIE

CHARLIE WAS ONE TOUGH, CANTANKEROUS, SARCASTIC old coot with whom to deal—much of the time. The rest of the time he just ignored you. Many of the other commercial travellers I knew hated to call on him—some simply refused to. When salesmen would get together at night at a hotel, we'd often discuss our toughest calls. Charlie was always near the top of everyone's list. I liked the guy, though, and I want to tell you why.

I've always operated on the premise that I don't care whether a customer likes me or not. If I could get their business, that meant they respected me, and that was more important. At the time, Charlie was supervisor for the five stores his company owned. At the store he managed and worked out of, purchasing for all the stores went through him.

The first time I called on him for Blackwood Marketing, I told him that I would visit every Friday morning at 9:00 a.m. Charlie laughed. Every Friday morning at 9:00 a.m., I walked through the door, and soon he was buying product from me. It wasn't long before I was calling on all their five stores in the St. John's area every Friday morning. I'd start at Charlie's, count the stock of our product in his warehouse on a spreadsheet, then go to the other stores and add their numbers.

I'd do up a recommended order in my car and take it back to

Charlie. It wasn't long before he started placing a weekly order—right after my late morning call. I'm sure at first he double-checked my numbers with his stores to make sure I was not trying to sell him a "bill of goods." I believe he was impressed with my dependability or honesty.

One Friday morning I walked in at 9:00 a.m., and Charlie, who was at the service counter, said loudly, in front of the staff and a couple other salesmen, "I need neither watch nor calendar. It must be 9:00 a.m., on Friday morning, because here comes Laurie."

The next time that I came in after checking all his stores on our products and doing up a suggested order, he said to me with an impatient edge to his voice, "Here's a purchase order. How about you write the order up? I don't have time for this every Friday." I did, and the trip after that he just pointed me to the top purchase order, already signed, and I wrote my own orders. There's nothing worth more than trust and nothing worth its betrayal.

But the thing that I will always remember about Charlie happened in the first year I called on him. I had taken on some lines and come to Newfoundland to get established. My wife and daughter were back in New Brunswick, waiting for our house to sell so I could move them. I was sleeping at my brother-in-law's house, in his rec room, and sometimes at the houses of dealers I knew when on the road. Money was tight.

I started in August month, and my entire month's sales came to $43,000. My commission for the month came to a little over $800. I spent that much in gas travelling the province that month, not to mention my meals, hotel rooms, car payment, phone, and all the commitments to the household in New Brunswick. It was brutal as I slid into debt.

Slowly, things picked up as dealers got to know and trust me. On the first week in December, I decided I had to go home for Christmas, although I couldn't afford to. I hadn't seen my family since July 30.

Our last truck to Newfoundland from our warehouse in Halifax was due to leave the end of the second week in December and be delivered the week before Christmas. Nobody wanted much product, as this was a slow period and many took inventory at year end and wanted their stock as low as possible. It was going to be a very thin Christmas—and I wouldn't even get my commission cheque until January.

As I was driving across the island on Friday of the second week, running for the ferry, I got a call from our order desk. There would be no truck. We didn't even have a quarter of a load. My boss agreed that if I could sell enough to fill the truck by that night, then they would send it. I worked the phone and couldn't get anything. The first call I made was to Charlie. He was grumpy.

"I haven't got time for this right now. Call me back in a few hours."

I called everyone else I knew and got nothing. Two or three hours later, I called Charlie, to tell him not to bother, as there would not be a truck coming.

"You're too late calling," he barked at me. "I've already ordered what I need."

"From us?" I asked.

"Some," he told me.

"How many lifts?" I asked.

"I don't know," he said, sounding annoyed. "I gave them a list of the things I needed and told them to send whatever quantities it takes to fill the truck. I'm busy. Goodbye."

"Thank you, Charlie. Merry Christmas." He was already gone off the line. Three-quarters of a truckload because he knew that *I* needed it! I had to pull over to the side of the road for a minute.

I've told that story to a few people. There aren't many who knew him that would believe me. I moved back to the mainland a few years later, but every time in Newfoundland I'd go to see him.

Charlie retired with well over fifty years in the hardware industry—all of it with the one employer. He didn't get his fifty-year Estwing Gold Hammer due to some politics or a mix-up, so I called in a couple of favours from friends in the industry and got it for him. I flew over and presented it to him at his house.

I don't suppose many would believe this, either, but he felt and reacted the same way I did the day he gave me a full truckload for Christmas. Charlie died and was buried just a month before I moved back to Newfoundland in 2013. I didn't get to say goodbye. I regret that, and you can believe that, too. There was a man who came to my rescue when I needed it most, and that's all you really need to say about any man, isn't it? RIP—Charlie.

KEVIN

I LIKED HIM FROM THE FIRST TIME I MET HIM. HE INTER-
viewed me for a position with Home Hardware at a Tim Hortons,
sure! A pickup truck pulled into the parking lot, and this big, slow-
walking country boy got out and ambled in and over to my table.

Having been around the business world for many years, I'd met
too many slick, big-city salespeople—the kind from "away" who talk
in patronizing tones about the quaintness of your area. You know—
the fast-talking kind with whom a store owner will be polite but never
completely trust. Kevin, however, was the real McCoy.

We talked that day about trucks, the farming and fishing indus-
tries, his hometown of Souris, Prince Edward Island, dealers who we
both knew, and of course his family. Then we got around to hardware.
A couple of coffees and a lot of conversation later, we left, going our
separate ways. I knew he would call me back, as he had promised. He
did, and I got the job.

Over the next three years, we spent countless hours together, driving from one end of the east coast to the other—meeting prospective
dealers, doing presentations, "mending fences, and putting out fires."
In the three years we worked together, it was either twenty or twenty-
one new stores we recruited for the Home Hardware Co-op—and more
fences fixed and fires extinguished than that company will ever know.

Old enough to be his father, I thought of him as a son—a smart, successful son whom I was proud to work with. Kevin had that special touch with the dealers. With his retail experience, they could relate to him, and with his style, they trusted him.

I can't remember how many store owners told me that Kevin was the best salesperson they ever had call on them.

Kevin drove a Nissan, most times, which I always referred to as his rusty Datsun. I drove an Audi, which he jokingly called just a pretentious Volkswagen. I always wanted to do the driving, not because of the car, but because I am deaf in my left ear. Sitting on the passenger's side, I have difficulty hearing the driver.

We'd be driving along in silence, sometimes, thinking about a meeting we just had, and out of the blue Kevin would pretend to turn on the radio and launch into a Johnny Cash song, "Folsom Prison Blues," or in his best Boomer Gallant start announcing a horse race: "Heeeeeeere they come! They're off and trotting . . ."

Kevin could also do very precise impersonations of dealers and others with whom we worked. He had a great ear for sound and would say the most unexpected things in the familiar voices of people we knew. I told him, "I bet you imitate me when I'm not around." He leaned in and, lowering his voice, made some smart-aleck remark. I forget what the words were, but he had my trademark mannerisms down pat.

At night in the hotels we'd eat, and occasionally, if we had a new dealer signed or if a presentation went really well, I'd have a drink of rum and Kevin would have a celebratory glass of wine. Then we'd walk back to our rooms and get on our computers to do our paperwork. There was no hanging around the bars or late nights drinking with Kevin.

He was kind. He was generous. He was funny. A man's character, however, is more important than his personality or what he might pretend to be. Kevin was a straight shooter and a family man. There were three women in his life of whom he often spoke—his wife and his two daughters. They were all he wanted, all he needed.

A few weeks before I finished with the company—and the last time that I travelled with him—we met up in Bridgetown, Nova Scotia. Fittingly, at the Tim Hortons. Since my contract period was nearly up, Kevin had some parting gifts for me. We sat outside at a picnic table, under the fragrant blossoms of an apple tree, and drank our coffees. Of my many memories of Kevin, it is, although bittersweet, my favourite. It was a long, quiet drive going back to Yarmouth alone.

Road warriors, like Kevin and I were, got used to those trips— those long hours—driving two or three thousand kilometres a week. "We're building," he used to say, "this great company of ours." We'd work a different town, and often a different province, each day. I can still see him lean in (imitating me) and almost hear him say, "I need to call Judy. Why don't you drive for a while? Wouldn't you like to drive a good car—for a change?"

As I write this, I have just received news that Kevin has passed away. I wish I could have known you longer, Kevin. Godspeed, old son.

THE RED TIE

I SOMETIMES WORE A RED TIE WITH A BLUE OR BLACK SUIT, and that evening as I was bounding up the stairs with my suitcase at the Atlantic Host Hotel in Bathurst, New Brunswick, I was so attired. Travelling on business, I stayed there often. I noticed a slim man, similarly dressed, coming down, and so I moved to the right to let him pass.

As he was abreast of me, he suddenly stopped, reached out, and gripped my arm.

"You are coming to the meeting, no?" he asked with a wide smile.

I looked up and into the face of Jean Chrétien. He was on a tour of local Liberal associations, running for the leadership of the Liberal Party of Canada. I was travelling for a hardware distributor and had no connection with the party. I explained this to him. He told me about the meeting, being held in a few minutes, and said, "You look like a good Liberal—you wear the red tie. You come in. I will speak, you know? And maybe you can find it interesting. You would vote for me in an election, no?"

"Certainly," I said, having long admired Chrétien as a cabinet minister in Pierre Trudeau's government, "but I am not a delegate. Will they let me in?"

"For sure," he said. "You will be with me."

I said I would attend. He said he was going to make a call and would be back up in five minutes. I put my suitcase in my room, combed my hair, and went back. My timing was perfect, and as I arrived at the meeting room door, Chrétien bounded back up the stairs, and we walked in together. The whole group turned as one to look as we entered.

He picked up a pamphlet off a table by the door and autographed it across his picture on the front. Then he found me a seat, patted me on the shoulder, and went to the front.

"If anyone asks," he said conspiratorially, "we are together."

I could see people whispering to each other, wondering who I was. This was a closed meeting, not a public one, so I assumed they thought I was a friend or rich donor. Jean spoke, in his usual folksy, emotional way. The crowd applauded wildly. He had them in the palm of his hand. I couldn't help but think what a great salesman he would make.

When it was over, he was swamped with people asking questions and getting autographs. I stayed for a few minutes, but wanting to have supper and having paperwork yet to do, I got up to slip away.

As I rose, it caught his eye, and from the front of the room, he waved and said, "Good night, Laurie, don't forget what we have agreed." The crowd turned to look as I held up my thumb and nodded. I suppose some wondered what multi-million dollar deal we had agreed to. I walked back to my room feeling a whole lot more important than I had any right to.

Chrétien won the leadership and the subsequent federal election and became prime minister. I haven't seen him since, but I have his autographed picture in my office.

And yes, Jean, I honoured our agreement.

TEN-DOLLAR BILL ON THE FLOOR

IT WAS MY FIRST WEEK AS NIGHT CREW MANAGER AT A supermarket, and I worked like a dog to see that the store looked as good as grand opening day—every morning. At night we'd fill the shelves and face the product across any "holes" so the store didn't look picked over. Then we'd do price changes, tag sale items, sweep and mop the floor—every morning.

We had only a small truckload to process on Thursday night that week, so we got through early. I sent the boys home before the normal time and intended to wait until the day crew arrived before going home myself. The store looked perfect. At about 7:30 a.m., I was startled as I looked up from my paperwork at the office desk and saw the area supervisor, Hank, coming into the office.

We always left the "out" door unlocked at night due to fire and emergency concerns. Although it had no outside handle, if you worked there you knew that you could stand to the side and, gripping the metal frame around the glass firmly, you could open it. So, I wasn't shocked to see him, but I was surprised when he told me he had already been around the store and it looked good.

"Just one thing," he told me. "There's a $10 bill on the floor down near the back." In the 1960s, that was almost a day's pay for a guy like me. He said he hadn't picked it up, and if I could find it, then it was mine. Curious, since I knew I hadn't dropped it, and I had checked the store over quite well before going up to the office, I went down to have a look.

I walked every aisle, some of them twice, but I saw no money. I did notice that one of the boys had brought out a crate of eggs just before he left and forgot to put them in the dairy counter. Since we kept eggs refrigerated, I put them in the counter and took the empty box out back. I had another quick look around, but there was no $10 bill.

When I got back to the office, Hank was grinning, and he asked if I found the money. That's when it hit me. Fifteen cartons of eggs in the box at sixty-some cents a carton equals about $10.

"Yes sir," I said, "I found it."

"Where is it now?"

"I put it in the dairy counter, Hank."

He smiled and handed me a $10 bill.

"This is yours," he said. "Product is money. If that was an actual $10 bill on the floor, no one would have left it there. If you think of all product that you touch as money, a lot less will get damaged or go bad and have to be thrown out."

Lesson learned—in a painless way. Soon thereafter I was promoted to assistant manager in another store and later to store manager. I never forgot that lesson, and my "shrinkage" percentage in inventory was always well below chain average.

I never forgot Hank, either, and more than from any of the courses I later took in management and economics, I learned from Hank how to be a retailer. An amazing friend and teacher for whom I would have done anything, Hank did more than that for me.

FOR HEATHER IN LA

HEATHER HAD A RATHER QUIET CHILDHOOD IN HER small rural community. At age thirteen, though, this willowy blonde with eyes as warm and blue as the Caribbean Sea got "saved" and at sixteen fell in love with the widowed preacher. A stunning beauty by now, she joined the choir and did volunteer work with the church's social services department. She dated no one. She loved only the pastor, and at eighteen they married. "He was a gift from God," she said, when at nineteen she gave birth to a son—the spitting image of his forty-year-old father.

After the marriage, though, her husband seemed to lose interest in her—or perhaps he rededicated himself to his church work. She doted on Jeremy as Bill grew more and more distant. Soon they hardly talked at all as he pursued "the Lord's work" and seemed to spend all his time praying or visiting his "flock."

She became mother and father to her son. She was the one who spoke out when he was bullied in school. She encouraged him to join the art and drama clubs. She never missed a show or a performance. It was fine with her that he was more artistic than athletic. His father, when he spoke at all, suggested the boy try more "manly" pursuits.

Their only child, she loved him dearly, and she nearly came apart when he took his own life at twenty-one. Heather had absolutely no idea that he was gay until the funeral. His friends flew, hitchhiked, drove, or biked in from LA, where he had been living, to the service in Wisconsin. There must have been thirty of them, and they all tented in her backyard.

Bill was totally unaware that many of these nice young men and women who came were "the worst kind of sinners." Had he known, he would surely have driven them all away.

Heather recognized at once that they were so like her son—kind, considerate, gentle—and she said it was only when she saw two guys kissing that it all fell into place.

"My face went red. It hit me like a ton of bricks," she told me. "I was so embarrassed and heartbroken that I hadn't known." Now she knew. Knew why he'd never had a steady girl and why he did not want to be a preacher. Knew why he hadn't come home often to visit. She wouldn't tell Bill until after the funeral.

Then Jeremy's boyfriend, James, came riding in on a Harley, parked, and walked straight over to Heather. He'd never met her but knew her from the picture Jeremy had on their dresser. They hugged and comforted each other for a long time. Jeremy's suicide note was written to James. He gave it to Heather. It asked him to go and say goodbye to his mom. "Tell Mom I wish I didn't have to do this, but I can't continue to live a lie. Tell her she's the first and only one I ever loved—until you, James."

So while Bill worked on the funeral arrangements in his office, Heather was outside with her late son's friends—talking about him, of his dreams, his fears, his hopes, and singing the songs he loved. An impromptu outdoor wake it was, with guitars, tambourines, and a banjo— his friends dancing and celebrating his life.

The day after the funeral, James suggested that Heather move to LA. It didn't take long to convince her. Her husband, Bill, was in a state of shock when she said goodbye. She got up on the back of that motorcycle carrying everything she cared about—a few mementoes, pictures, and Jeremy's urn in a backpack—and then just rode away.

I haven't seen Heather in years, but even without the occasional picture she posts on Facebook now, I'd know she is still beautiful. She's divorced, remarried, and she still works, part-time, with James at the community outreach centre he runs in LA. They're helping young people—kids who still flock to the west coast, gay or straight, and need a place to live, a job of work, and guidance in finding their own way in life.

Back in Wisconsin, preacher Bill is retired but still leaves literature in strangers' doors. The words on the leaflets condemn to "everlasting fire and torment" those who live like Jeremy. He truly believes that his late son will suffer for eternity, as will his ex-wife—as divorce is against God's will, too.

Heather, Jeremy, and James, however, have all found peace—each in their own way.

There's Always Hope

SHE'S A KIND, CARING, WARM-HEARTED WOMAN, AND she wears body armour of steel, wrapped in barbed wire, so you can't get close enough to hurt her.

She has a heart-wrenching backstory. Born to a single Aboriginal mother and her black boyfriend, she was given up for adoption. At that time and place, few except affluent white people could afford to adopt a child. Even fewer had the courage to adopt a non-white or mixed-race child—no matter how attractive or lovable they might be.

So she ended up with the Children's Aid. That government agency compensated families who would take children in and provide some kind of a home for them. Some kids got lucky and found a kind, nurturing family, became an integral part of it—and often were later adopted by them. Many did not.

It was common for these kids—those who lost out in the adoption lottery, especially if they were older—to be sent to live with farm families. There's always lots of work to do on a farm and often too few hands. Some of these families were kind. Some were not—and treated these unpaid kids like slaves. She went to a farm.

Many of them spent all their after-school evenings, their weekends, and their school vacations working. Unless you've spent a summer out in the blazing sun making hay and hoeing by hand those endless rows of vegetables, you really don't know the definition of hard work. If you were mistreated or shown no love or little appreciation for what you did, you might begin to understand how she felt.

Then when she started to mature, the farmer's son decided to use her in a different way—tried to practise on her the positions he'd read about in men's adult magazines. She ran away. They brought her back. She ran again. Finally, she was old enough and they could no longer force her to go back. She struck out on her own. She found a job, found a place to live, and, despite her earlier trauma, was able to develop adult relationships and have boyfriends. She never married, though, and had no children.

She was about forty and working night shift at a restaurant when I met her. I was often up very late or sleepless, and I'd go for a drive and pick up a coffee there. If I had my dog with me, he'd get a free treat. She'd take great pleasure in insulting customers she knew well. Once every shift she'd give out a free coffee. She called it her Asshole of the Night Award.

One night I got a free one early in her shift. I suggested she should wait until later in the night to make sure she was awarding the rightful winner. She told me, "Then you would win every night. There couldn't possibly be a bigger one." On some nights it was very quiet, and if no one was in the lineup behind me, we'd talk.

A tall, dark, attractive woman, I wondered if she had a lot of men hitting on her. Yes, she told me. Did it bother her? "No, except for one old man who comes through here and keeps asking me out." How old was he? I wanted to know. "*Real* old," she told me, "about sixty-five, I'd say." I think she suddenly realized that I was about the same age (real old), and she added this disclaimer, "But it wouldn't bother me if it were you . . . you're still doable!"

Someday an exceptional man will find a way past that barbed wire, then through the cold steel armour, and touch her heart. No matter what cards you're dealt, no matter how rigged the game is, if you can keep your sense of humour, there's always Hope.

— CHAPTER 3 —

ANIMALS:
THE QUICK AND THE DEAD

We interact constantly with other humans and almost as often with animals. In some cases it could be argued that many of us interact more with animals than we do with each other. People who live alone but with a pet or three, birdwatchers, dog catchers, and animal shelter workers all fall into that category.

We don't live by the rules and customs of the animal world, but we insist they live by ours—or else. This animal-human relationship can make for some interesting stories. Here are some of mine.

Moose Hunting

I'VE LIVED IN THREE DIFFERENT COMMUNITIES IN NEW-foundland, and at two of those places I have had moose come into the yard and browse, seemingly unbothered by my presence. At the third house the moose went up the side into the neighbour's yard and sampled our foliage from over the fence. If you drive across the island and don't see one, rest assured a dozen or two saw you from the edge of the woods.

There are an estimated 110,000–150,000 moose here now. Some say it peaked at 150,000 a few years back and the population is declining. Others say there are many more moose than these estimates. How would you count moose that are spread all across this huge island? You can't. The fir and spruce will hide them in winter, and those trees along with the deciduous ones will hide them in summer. All you can do, I suppose, is *try* to count the number in a few random square kilometres and somehow extrapolate the average number to the entire province.

In any event, it is a huge population of an animal, not native, that got to this number from four (4) animals which were introduced here in 1904. I've not hunted moose here. The only place I have hunted them is in New Brunswick, where ours originally came from. It was a dismal experience and cured me of the desire to hunt.

It was 1985, and I went with a guide and a couple other guys just outside Fundy National Park in Albert County.

I was told that all I needed to bring was a sleeping bag, toilet tissue, and two twenty-fours of beer. I arrived at the camp in the morning, and we commenced to drink a few beers before starting—as the boys were "a little dry" from the night before.

Then they ate. I can't eat in the morning, so I sipped on a cold one while the boys had a big feed of bacon and eggs washed down with beer. On my empty stomach, the alcohol went straight to my head. We got out of the camp well before noon—or perhaps that should read, "Well . . . we got out of the camp before noon."

Next we commenced to walk—through woods, briar thickets, marshes, meadows, and swamps—and I know it must have been only a mirage, but I swear we crossed a desert in the heat of late afternoon. Dry? Funny how having nothing in your stomach but a half-dozen beers will make you dry. Finally we made it back to camp, with a compass and just enough light to find our way. Then the boys got serious about drinking. My first twenty-four was gone about 10:00 p.m., and now it was time to eat.

I don't remember what they cooked up, but it was good and filling. I had such a buzz going and it was so hot by the wood stove that I got stomach sick and went outside and lost it all. By then all the food was gone, and not wanting to have the beer beat me, I broke into my second twenty-four.

The next day was a repeat of the same. We marched over muskeg and mountains, walked around windfalls and waterfalls, but we never got within a day of a moose. We saw a lot of beds, and we encountered a few tracks in the wet mud, but they had cobwebs across them.

By the second night I was starving. Apparently the second night they would normally have moose liver from the first kill, so there wasn't much food to be had. It might have been fried farts and wild mushrooms, for all I know. I was too drunk by 10:00 p.m. to tell. Whatever it was, I lost it outside again. Then I drank some more beer, and when I had a full case of empties, I crashed in my sleeping bag.

I was due to leave the next morning, although the rest of the guys were staying for another day. I slept right through their leaving and woke up about noon—starving and as dry as a nomad's fart. I gathered up my sleeping bag, two boxes of beer bottles, and my toilet tissue, and drove into Alma, where I had a big breakfast.

The only good thing about the trip was I didn't even open up the package of toilet paper. I was able to put it back on the shelf of the store I owned. Food, of course, has to pass through the digestive system before toilet paper is required.

Obituary for Snagglepuss Pike

She was, without question, the scrawniest, scratch-ingest, cross-eyedest cat I'd ever seen.

It was the winter of 2001. We had just moved into a 150-year-old house. The previous owners apparently didn't know that the basement was the local flophouse for a large community of mice. There were moles, voles, deer mice, field mice, house mice, sighted mice, likely three blind mice, and possibly some nice mice. *Nice mice?*

Scratch that last one. My wife informs me that there are no nice mice.

We wanted them all gone, quickly.

Snagglepuss, then named Phyllis, was somewhere between age two and four and living at the Yarmouth SPCA. They had many friendly cats of different sizes and colours, some of them too contented to get up and come over, yet I was drawn to this, the most unadoptable one available. She was going to be there for a very long time—or worse.

We had cats in my childhood, and Dad used to say if you want a good mouser, get the scrawniest, skinniest, ugliest cat you can find . . . and Snaggers sure had that lean and hungry look. I took her home, and she fought me every inch of the way. Then she went to work and did her job with a vengeance. Within weeks the basement was rodent-free.

We don't know how, but over time her crossed eyes straightened.

She put on some weight. Snags was a troubled cat, fearless with mice but scared of people.

If you would approach her at eye level—down on the floor—okay, but if you bent to pick her up, the claws and teeth changed your mind quickly. She never learned to trust us. She never got over her fear. She must have had an awfully abused and frightening kittenhood.

She lived in three provinces with us in her fourteen to sixteen years. She had no youngsters. An inside cat, she was "unemployed" for the last few years, as she had taken her duties seriously and worked herself out of a job.

Snaggers took sick, but I assumed it was stress as we were moving again, and the whole house was in turmoil. She quit eating and drinking. Then my wife found blood in her urine.

I took her to the vet that morning, and the diagnosis was bad, the choice singular. Under sedation was the first time she didn't try to scratch me when I reached out to her. She blinked her eyes as I stroked her fur, and then she was gone, as quickly as she had come into our lives.

When I walked out, with the empty cage, I could feel the other pet owners' eyes on me—expecting me to cry, I s'pose. I marched bravely on, like you would. When I got to the car, I drove around for an hour, trying to compose myself before going home.

I hope she is now without pain and fear, somewhere where there are no mean people, where the dogs are small and respectful, and the whole place is overrun with fat, slow mice.

RIP—Snaggie . . . you poor little girl. Can't nobody ever hurt you now!

STUFFED ANIMALS

I HAVE A STUFFED BARRED OWL AT HOME WHICH HAD flown into the side of a tractor-trailer near Moncton and died instantly. The driver stopped and walked back to make sure the owl was dead. A beautiful bird, almost twenty inches long in shades of grey and brown except for its yellow beak, he thought it was a shame to leave it at the side of the road for the scavengers to tear apart. He took it to a taxidermist the next morning and had it mounted. I bought it from the taxidermist.

I've had this owl for about thirty years, and it has been with me in three provinces and in eight houses. I would never shoot an owl or any other animal for a trophy and have no respect for those who would do so. I have hunted, and fished, and I would eat or share with others what I took. I no longer hunt. As I get older, I put more value on life—any life. When I go in the woods now, depending on the season, I might carry a .22 rifle or a shotgun—in case I run into a rabid animal or a hungry coyote. I carry a camera as a way to remember the walk and any creatures I encounter. I haven't had to use a firearm, though.

I also have a stuffed coyote that my neighbour killed up in back of his house. With small children and chickens around, he was not going to take the risk. He has since passed away, but every time I look at the coyote, I remember his friendship and the good times we had. I also have the head of a spike-horned, white-tail deer. The deer was shot by a hunter who used the meat and gave the head to a taxidermist. Here's the story the taxidermist said was told to him.

"It was the last day of the season—my last chance to fill the freezer for winter. It was just coming dark, and I was on a woods road heading back out to my car. I stopped at a bend in the road, sat on the trunk of a fallen tree, and smoked a cigarette.

"I was about to get up again when around the corner came two deer, a young buck, and a doe following, coming full tilt, taking big bounds as if a pack of coyotes were in pursuit. I raised my rifle at the last minute, and at the top of his leap I squeezed the trigger. He came down and dropped almost at my feet. The doe leapt sideways into the woods."

A couple of years ago, a neighbour dropped in and saw the deer head mounted on the wall in my office. He seemed quite taken with it, as we have no deer here in Newfoundland. Studying it closely for a few minutes, he lit a cigarette and turned to me and said, "I figure that deer was at the top of his leap and going real fast when he cashed in."

My mouth flew open, and all I could think of saying was, "How the hell would you know that?"

"Well," he said, after taking a long draw on his smoke, "he's high up on your wall, and he had to be going wonderful fast. He came partways through it, sure."

A Dog's Breakfast

I RECENTLY BOUGHT A BAG OF DRY DOG FOOD. IT'S A WELL-known brand, and the slogan on the bag says, THE TASTE YOUR DOGS WILL LOVE! My dog, Harley, hates it—and every other kind of dry dog food I bring home. Do you s'pose these pet food folks use the finest, freshest cuts of meat, supplemented with added vitamins and minerals, to keep my dog healthy and make him beg for his supper? Not likely. And the cheaper cuts of meat and by-products go into hot dogs and bologna, right? So, do you even want to think about what they put in dog food? No? I didn't think so.

None of this "care and attention" to the animal's taste buds and nutritional health has any effect on him. He wants what people eat. About the only human food he won't eat is turnip—smart dog. Of course, most of what we eat is not dry. So, I thought, *Does he simply like his food wet?* I tried dry dog food with water poured over it. The dog food turned to mush, he wouldn't touch it, and it dried out and hardened into a round disc, taking on the shape of his dish.

A few days later, I took this disc outdoors and threw it to him like a Frisbee. He ran to it, but he wouldn't chew on it or bring it back. I looked away for a few minutes, and when I glanced back, he was trying to bury it.

Anything off the table, however—even bread—he will stand at

the dish and eat it till it's all gone. He'll eventually eat the dry dog food, but he picks up a couple pieces of the kibble at a time and carries them into the living room where I am watching TV.

He'll drop them on the floor, look at me, and then pick up each piece individually and eat it. Like a kid who hates peas, he wants you to know that he hates it, but he's doing his best to get it down.

Sometimes he'll just sit and stare, unblinking, at me. Then he'll give a big sigh and get up and walk away. I've never had a dog before that did this. I think he learned that expression from my wife. He hasn't got the eye roll down yet.

If there's any gravy in the fridge, I'll pour a bit over the dry dog food and he'll gulp it all down. Ditto for the liquid left in a sardine can. Just pour it on his food and the food's gone.

What I'd like to know is: On which dogs do these dog food manufacturers test their food? Is it on stray starving dogs that the SPCA picks up? Or is it on dogs that have just run the entire Iditarod Dogsled Race for twelve days without a meal and are so hungry they would chew the leg off the Lamb of God if they could get close enough?

There's Neither "R" in June

"SO WHAT?" SAYS YOU. "THERE'S NO 'Q' IN CUCUMBER, either."

But my point is that you can't eat a rabbit in any month with neither "R" in it. The June month has no "R." So, from May to August, rabbits are forbidden. I wouldn't kill any animal that I don't intend to eat—unless of course it's about to kill me. And these cute little devils wouldn't harm an earthworm—although they have eaten everything else that dared stick its head above ground in my garden.

Even if it was open season—and they were fit to eat, according to our customs—how could you look at these handsome little beasts and then squeeze the trigger? I can walk within a few feet of them and they hardly even interrupt their browsing. We have a number of these bold-as-brass little beggars around every day, but they usually come out of the woods one at a time. I am so familiar with them now that I can tell them apart, and not just by size.

I had a bare area in the yard that I sowed to white clover last year, and this is their favourite end of the buffet. They also like the leaves of the dogberry trees, and they like anything I planted in the vegetable garden. Since I can't and won't shoot the little rascals, I thought I might try a trap.

I've had a harmless box trap set up for the last month. My plan was to trap them one by one and then relocate them to an area far from my home place. I've baited the trap with fresh lettuce, carrots, and cabbage, and reading on the Internet that they like apples, I tried them, too.

Now, as you know, you aren't going to get any of those exotic things in Newfoundland in the May month or any other month without going to the Sobeys or the Dominion store—sometimes not even then. The rabbits turned up their noses—or twitched them—and then went on back to filling their faces on my homegrown stuff.

How stunned am I? Why do I buy these expensive treats for the little bandits in hopes that I can salvage a paltry few low-quality vegetables? Even at the best of times, what more can you expect from this barren, cold, glacial till? Most people will subtract the cost of their seeds from the value of their harvest and come out ahead. Me? I've gone further in the hole by providing expensive but ineffective bribes to these hungry hopping hoodlums.

No, it's no use. I can't catch 'em and I won't shoot 'em. I should take some pictures, though. They're so tame that if I point a camera at them they'd like as not come over and sniff to see if it's fit to eat. I'm sure they'd pose for you if you knew the rabbit words for "Say cheese."

I could fence in the whole yard or at least the vegetable garden. But what odds? Let the furry little friggers eat their fill. I know I'm getting soft in my old age, but that started a long time ago with a story my daughter told me.

She loves animals and has rescued a few over the years. As a child she even rescued and bottle-fed an abandoned baby rabbit, but we set him free when he was old enough. We also had cats and dogs at home when she was growing up. She never had a real pet rabbit, though.

When she was a teenager, she was walking with a male friend in Manuels, CBS, and they walked past a house with a sign in the window which read, RABBITS FOR SALE.

They went back, knocked, and she asked if she could see them. While the man was gone to get them, I'm sure she was thinking about the cost of a cage, and where to buy rabbit food, and how cute and cuddly they were. Buddy came back with a brace of skinned wild rabbits!

"They're already cleaned," he said as he tried to pass them to her.

You s'pose that wouldn't tear out the heart of a young maid who loves animals?

And when Grandpa Pike thinks about killing a wild rabbit, he sees only the look that must have been on her face. I can't do it.

So, I guess I'll let the celery-chomping, carrot-crunching, pea-poaching, lettuce-lifting, garden-destroying, seven–sided little off-spring of the son of Satan live, so I will. They're cute little demons—no mistake.

CATS

I'VE OWNED LOTS OF CATS. CORRECTION. NOBODY OWNS a cat. A cat will either take to you or avoid you, and there is nothing you can do to change that. If they don't like or trust you, then they'll just leave you alone. Cats choose which "pride" they want to join. If they adopt you, be thankful, but never attempt to show them who's the boss.

If it is an outdoor cat, don't try to make it an indoor one, and vice versa. An indoor cat will eat when it's hungry, sleep when it's sleepy, and come when you call only if it is hungry and it thinks you have food. If an indoor cat knew how to use a can opener, and clean out a litter box, it would, most times, just ignore you—unless it likes company when it sleeps.

In the wild cat species, one cat in the pride will stay awake and keep watch—for prey or enemies. Some cats will disappear from your bed the minute they think you are asleep—likely a throwback to their wild nature. They sense it's their turn to get up and keep watch.

Outdoor cats want to hunt. If you don't want your cat killing birds and rodents, you will not be happy with one. You can't control the urge. If you fill the cat up with gourmet food before it goes out, it will still kill. Perhaps it's the thrill of the hunt.

Don't declaw your outside cat, either, or you will take away its first line of defence. You can bell your cat. This will compromise its ability to kill birds, but it will also give its location away to enemies—like coyotes and dogs. Outdoor cats, if they could work a doorknob, wouldn't need you at all.

Unlike dogs, it is very difficult to teach tricks to a cat. I met a guy at a house party once, though, who claimed he had taught his cat to use the toilet.

"I'm not shittin' you," I believe were his exact words, "she'll sit on the toilet and do her Number Two."

I found that hard to believe, but then he went way over the top with, "Only thing is, half the time she forgets to flush."

A few beers later, he was telling us that he knew how to "play" the cat. We all laughed, and then he offered to play the host's cat. After assuring her that her cat would come to no harm, she agreed that he could demonstrate.

First he soothed the cat by stroking its fur and whispering sweet nothings, then he positioned the cat against his side, sort of holding him with his elbow. The cat's head pointed down and back and the tail up and front. He didn't hurt the cat, but he needed to get him a little annoyed, he said, in order for it to vocalize. With alternately squeezing the cat's belly with his elbow and gently nibbling on the tip of its tail, he coaxed some interesting sounds from his instrument. A sound not unlike that which a damaged bagpipe might emit.

I still don't believe the little bugger's story about his cat flushing the toilet. However, after hearing a truly *moving* version of "Amazing Grace," on the cat, I have to admit that anything is possible.

Muttley and Sheba

I ACQUIRED MY FIRST DOG WHEN I WAS IN MY EARLY THIR-ties, although I am partial to cats. A cat will keep the rodents at bay, and most of them are too smart to tangle with a skunk or porcupine. Dogs, not so much. My first dog was Muttley, named after a cartoon character of my childhood. We got him as company for my girlfriend when we were living out in the country in Yarmouth County. I was away on my job most weeknights. Then the lady left.

He was a good dog. I trained him to stay on our side of the road, and he'd run the woods and the fields but wouldn't cross the road. My neighbour Gordon came over to plow a garden plot for me and ran over him. He limped away, and Gordon got him some food and water, as I was away. Gord had no other vehicle than his farm tractor, so he couldn't take Muttley to a vet.

I took him, and amazingly nothing was broken, just some bad bruising. The vet gave me some pills to mix in with his food. I don't remember if they were antibiotics or for pain. In any event, he took it well. He'd been backed over by the big rear wheel of a farm tractor, and yet he recovered in a couple of weeks.

You could still see the tread pattern on his rump so clearly for weeks after, that a good forensics person could have identified the vehicle responsible. Poor old puppy dog. Since my girlfriend had left me to go back to Toronto, and I hated living alone, I moved to an apartment in Halifax, and I had to give him away.

My next dog was Sheba, a mixed breed we acquired at the pound after I was married. Again, living in the country, we got her as protection and company for my wife, Katie, when I was away at my travelling job. Sheba was a docile dog. She wouldn't bark to warn of noises or strangers in the night.

We used to joke that if anyone broke in while we were away, she'd show them where all our valuables were. She'd come when you called, and sit, and beg, and all the other things you teach a dog to do. She wanted to please you, but she only really came alive if young children or teenagers came to visit.

One quiet moonlit night when I couldn't sleep, I looked out the window and saw some movement down by my car. Here were two young fellows, with a length of hose, trying to siphon fuel from my gas tank. At the time I didn't have a gun to scare them away with, and not knowing if they might be armed, I decided to call the police.

They got their gas and hurried on down the driveway to their car, which had run out of fuel right under the only streetlight for a mile. Ontario plates, but I couldn't make out the number. Apparently a couple of Maritimers and their old beat-up car, trying to make it home or back to their jobs in Upper Canada.

I thought about calling the cops back and telling them not to bother. I had a full tank, and they only took a couple gallons. After all, I'd done a few stupid things in my youth. They got a good head start on the cops. Two days later, the cops arrived. I figure the kids were already back in Toronto, even after having to stop every twenty-five miles or so for more gas.

What bothered me most about the whole thing was Sheba. I believe it was a trick of the light, and I know I'm a fool to think it, but as they were fumbling with the cap on their jerry can, I would swear I saw Sheba holding their siphon hose in her paws and sucking on it to get the gas started.

The Habits of Harley

Harley's about ten years old now, a cross between a Bernese mountain dog and a Labrador retriever—a Labernese. (We used to call mixed breeds like this Heinz 57s.) He is good-natured, loves kids, and never barks or whines, but he has other strange and sometimes annoying habits.

He gets more water on the floor than he does in his mouth when drinking from his dish. I've seen a few other dogs drink, and sure there are drips and drops, especially if they turn to look at you while drinking. With Harley it's a flood of water. We constantly have to mop or risk slipping in it.

Sometimes before he sits down on the floor, he will do a half-dozen turns—like a dog pirouette— before he sits. I could understand this if the surface were uneven, like a pile of loose blankets, and he were looking for the best way to lay flat. It's as if he is trying to find the best position for seeing everything in the room at once. He also seems to want his ass and his head facing you at the same time.

Dogs seem to enjoy turning their ass to you. A cat will face you, with her backside hidden when doing her thing at the litter box. Cats are discreet—and will cover their deed when done. Not a dog—at least not Harley. He goes outside, and we watch from the window so he doesn't wander off and to let him in when he's done.

Harley, like most dogs, will urinate first. He then trots across our lawn on a diagonal, for corner to corner, then starts a second diagonal of the other two corners. When he gets to where the lines intersect, he stops, knowing I suppose that he has reached the exact centre of the lawn. A surveyor wouldn't be much more accurate.

Slowly he turns, until his ass is facing us, and then hunches down and makes his deposit. Sometimes before he starts he'll look toward the house and adjust his ass, seemingly, to our view. When he stands back up, he turns to look at us, seeking approval, one supposes, makes a half-hearted scratch with his paw, pretending he's trying to cover it, and then runs around, tail wagging, delighted with his insult and deception.

I have a lot to learn about dogs.

When I was a child, I rode a bus to school. One Friday afternoon, one of the neighbours' young sons was sitting beside me, and his city friend in the window seat. The friend was coming to the country for the first time, to stay with our neighbours for the weekend. As the bus ground to a halt in front of their very long gravel driveway, a nanny goat came running down to meet the bus. The city boy looked excitedly at the country boy and exclaimed, "Is that your puppy dog!?" Everyone on the bus laughed. I know a little more about dogs than that, but my dog is about as strange as any I've known. He is my puppy dog, though.

— CHAPTER 4 —
LIFE'S LITTLE ANNOYANCES

Things that bother or irritate us we call annoyances. For example: That last mosquito in the tent which comes buzzing around, tormenting you just when you are about to go to sleep—and suddenly disappears after you have awoken the entire camp.

Or that little brat in the airline seat ahead of you who keeps turning around and sticking out his tongue—but smiles like a little angel when his parents turn and catch you finally returning his salutation. They look at you in disgust. What can you do—say he started it? These little annoyances won't ruin your life, but we feel we have to tell someone about them. Here are some of mine.

NINE OUT OF TEN DOCTORS RECOMMEND . . .

EVERY TIME I SEE AN AD WHERE NINE OF TEN DOCTORS recommend something, I have to wonder—what did the tenth one say?

"Well, I tried it on three of my patients, and the first one was pronounced dead within minutes, the second is comatose, and the third is suffering from headaches, nausea, vomiting, boils, fever, and a team of the best doctors from the Mayo Clinic is trying to determine why his ass fell off."

Was she was the only one who did not accept payment for endorsing the new product? If only ninety per cent of doctors agree with a course of treatment—or a particular medication—why do the others disagree? Do they believe it's dangerous or just ineffective?

Why do we allow doctors to recommend anything to the general public without seeing the patient? Why don't they give the names and addresses of the nine doctors who endorse the product? For all we know, these nine have all been convicted of malpractice and need every bit of income they can scrape together to pay their fines.

If the medical association firmly believes in a product or a course of action for an ailment, why doesn't the medical association *itself* do the recommending? Are they afraid of being sued? It would be nice to see their stamp of approval on products that they believe are the best—if, indeed, they believe it is possible to recommend one without examining the patient. If they won't endorse, then why do they allow their members to do it?

Nine chances out of ten we won't see a change any time soon.

Feeling Lonely in Newfoundland? Go for a Drive, Sure

A RE YOU VISITING, OR NEW HERE AND HAVEN'T MADE any friends yet? Fear not! The perfect way to meet people is to go for a drive. From the minute you get off the boat at Port aux Basques, you'll have company. There will be a car or big beefed-up pickup truck on your rear bumper all the way to St. John's. They don't seem to want to pass. They just want to occupy the space you are in—and right now!

If you hit a moose or stop suddenly for any other trivial reason, they will be right in the back seat with you. They won't let you get lonely. Same thing if you fly into town. Get in your rental, and these comforting individuals will accompany you all the way to your hotel. If for some reason they tire of you or decide to go elsewhere, fear not, another will slip right in to replace them and comfort you in your loneliness.

It's not only the men who are aggressive—the women are even worse. (No, I don't mean all those bay girls down on George Street— we all know what they're like, sure—I mean when driving.) The guys will just want to trade paint with you as they slide by, but the women will show you their nail polish by holding up one finger for you to appraise. What do you think of this colour, old man, luh? Luh!

The other thing to be constantly conscious of in Newfoundland is right-of-way. We take it seriously, like human rights and politics. If a Newfoundlander has the right-of-way or thinks he or she has the right-of-way, they will fight for it—die for it, if necessary.

Even if you are already into the turn, if there is a better than forty per cent chance that they can make it and/or escape death, they will take it.

Don't get me wrong, Newfoundlanders are the kindest people on earth—they'll give you the shirt off their back and then likely invite you home to choose a jacket to match. They'll jump into a burning car to save your life or even split their last beer with you. Don't take their right-of-way, though, or they'll run right over you. Don't be lonely. Go for a drive, sure.

YARD SALES

YOU SEE THEM EVERYWHERE IN THE SUMMERTIME. They might be advertised as garage sales or flea markets—and some churches and women's organizations still call them rummage sales. They are all different but all the same, in that somebody is trying to get rid of old junk they don't want—and make a dollar doing it. I've even held one myself.

I spent a whole day going through everything we owned, trying to eliminate things we no longer wanted. We were moving. I priced the items low. Two bucks for a set of three-wheel discs, two bucks for a pair of ice skates, and five for an old TV. We advertised for 9:00 a.m., and at seven, before we even had things put out, they were knocking on the door and parking on the lawn.

The first lady offered me a dollar for the discs, but she wanted all three. She said she only needed one but she'd take them all because the two left would be no good to anyone else. There's logic, eh? Next lady wanted the skates for her son and wondered if she could return them tomorrow if they didn't fit! The third old girl went up one side of me and down the other because our ad didn't say the TV was not flat-screen and she drove ten kilometres to get here.

I'll stop at the odd sale myself if I see something interesting from the road. A middle-aged couple were having one a few streets over, and I saw a hand-held vacuum cleaner on the table—the kind you use to clean out the car. I asked the husband if it worked. Yes, he told me, it worked fine last time he used it, this past summer.

Next I saw a jigsaw puzzle, and I asked if all the pieces were there. He checked with his wife, and they assured me that they were. As he was making change, he told me they were raising money for their church to help send an underprivileged kid to camp. I owed them $5 but told him to keep the change from the ten. I put my treasures in the trunk of the car and forgot about them for a week or so.

When I took them out, I discovered that the little electric motor was missing from the vacuum, and a small rodent had built a nest in its place. My wife told me later that evening that the puzzle contained pieces from at least two different puzzles. We threw both purchases in the garbage can.

Next day, I was at the mall with a friend, and I saw the yard sale couple in a store, shopping. I pointed them out and asked my friend if he knew them.

"Why yes," he told me, "that's Rev. and Mrs. Wilkins from my church."

I hope they got that kid to camp, and I hope he doesn't know what they did to get him there. Do you suppose a little deceit is justified for a worthy cause?

GET YOUR *OWN* FACEBOOK PAGE

O NE SIMPLE REASON. YOU DON'T KNOW WHO YOU'RE talking to. If a couple uses the same page (Jack and Jill Smith), there's only one way to find out to whom you're speaking. Ask.

I had a good friend—at least so I thought—whose wife was always posting about their fancy dinner parties, trips, and their condo in Florida or New York . . . who cares? I made some silly comment about the "rich and famous," and suddenly I'm "unfriended." I asked him about it next time we had coffee. He said his wife unfriended me. Grow some, buddy. Get your own page if you can't find any pants to put on in the morning.

Facebook can be a blessing and a curse. I talk to some people regularly whom I haven't seen since high school. When they post old pictures of the hometown or use a colloquial expression that I grew up with, I feel a connectedness. It's nice to see how people's lives turned out, too—people you liked or cared about so long ago. As you get older, you like to go back, and this is really the only way you can.

I spend too much time on Facebook, though. It takes time away from my writing, but sometimes it provides ideas for stories, too—like this one.

But be careful on Facebook. If you assume who's there, you'll get it wrong—and there are things you might say to a guy that you wouldn't say to his wife. You think it's Jack on there because they just posted a picture of a muscle car. So you go to chat and you write, "How they hanging?"

"Sagging, you mean?" Jill responds. How do you get out of that one? Do you say "not for long"? (Her husband just told you a month ago that she's getting implants.)

NOT A NEWFOUNDLANDER?

WHAT QUALIFIES YOU TO BE A NEWFOUNDLANDER and Labradorian? Is it when you were born, where you live, your ethnicity or race, or your accented speech?

Speech? I have been asked, many times, "Where are you from . . . *originally*?" When I respond with another question—"Why do you ask?"—as I usually do, I'm told, "Because you don't sound like we." So . . . how do Newfoundlanders sound?

Outside of Newfoundland, many Canadians think we all sound alike—that there is one Newfoundland accent. Yet from community to community there are distinct differences in pronunciations, colloquialisms, rapidity of speech, and other variances.

Someone from one bay may have difficulty understanding one from another bay. Those with a very good ear, however, can often tell which bay you are from, right down to the individual community. So . . . it's not a specific accented English that makes you a Newfoundlander.

Ethnicity or race? To me there's only one race—the human race. Anyone from Africa, Asia, or anywhere else who comes to live here and loves this place is a Newfoundlander. If they want to keep their bloodlines "pure," they had better not have youngsters. "Their" kids and "ours" will take care of that in the first generation. So . . . it's not race.

Where you live? There are Newfoundlanders everywhere on the face of the earth. People (workers) have been our biggest export after fish and newsprint. Many have not lived here for decades—or were born to Newfoundlanders elsewhere.

Many more work elsewhere, but maintain a residence here, while living "away" and will return here to retire. So . . . it's not where you live.

When you were born? There are those who say that unless you were born *here*, prior to one minute before midnight on March 31, 1949 (when Newfoundland joined Canada), then you're not a true Newfoundlander. The rest of us then must be mere Canadians? So . . . Newfoundlanders will cease to exist after all born before that date are dead and buried? Not on your life! So . . . it's not when you were born, either.

I was born in Newfoundland in 1944. My mother and numerous generations before her were born here. My father was the son of two Newfoundlanders and was born in Cape Breton, Nova Scotia, when his parents were "away"—his father working there. They moved back.

In 1948, my family moved to the mainland. I grew up there, and I was called a Newfoundlander or that other N-word which I don't like. I came back here in middle age and had to leave again chasing employment. This is now the third time I've moved back. So how am I not a Newfoundlander? Because I don't sound like ye?

Door-to-Door Science Salespeople

Y EARS AGO THERE WOULD BE FULLER BRUSH, WATKINS, and Rawleigh salespeople coming to the door on a regular basis. Add to that the encyclopedia salespeople and those selling magazine subscriptions, vacuum cleaners, greeting cards, and other products. It was a rare day when some peddler didn't arrive.

That's all gone now, except for the politics and religion salespeople. The politics ones you only see once every four years, but the religion ones are still quite persistent. Some of them are okay, like the Mormons, who are polite and respectful. If I have time, I talk with them and wish them well. Some of the others, though, are harder to handle.

If you show them the least bit of courtesy, they will insist on saving your soul. It doesn't matter if you didn't know it was lost, or even if you never knew you had one. Persistent? The trouble is, many of these people believe that the world was created 6,000 years ago. They deny everything from evolution, to global warming, to common sense. It's time that science fought back!

The solution? Simple—door-to-door science salespeople. After a bachelor's degree in any field of science, the graduate must do a year of "missionary" work. (If they are going on to a masters or doctorate, they could get a deferment, until their education is complete.) Let them get out there and counteract the damage some of these door-to-door religion salespeople are doing. They could travel in pairs, like the Mormons, to a distant community and go door to door educating us.

How would we pay for it? They could accept donations to science, and all funds exceeding their living expenses would go to a central foundation. We would make this entity tax-free—like churches. They could bring in more money by selling science books, chemistry sets, and fossils. They'd also leave pamphlets if no one was home, with titles like "Wake Up" or some such name—to shock people into facing reality.

The profits would go to holding free seminars, TV ads, and other educational programs to get people involved in saving the planet before it's too late. Sure, some people will pretend they aren't home. Some will sic the Doberman on them. Some will wave a firearm. Some will even come to the door stark naked to discourage them—but did any of that ever stop the religion salespeople? Not at my house.

NUMBER 13 AND OTHER SUPERSTITIONS

I HAVE A NUMBER OF SUPERSTITIONS. I UNDERSTAND THE logic of not walking under a ladder—especially if they're hauling up bricks, or if that tipsy painter has a poor grip on the Benjamin Moore.

I don't get the "not buying a broom in May" or "not letting a black cat cross your path." I don't get the "number 13" thing, either, but I respect it and am extra careful on a Friday-13 combo.

I will not stay in a hotel's room 13. Some try to fool us by starting their room numbers with 100, then 101, etc. I've got news—room 113 is room 13 *with a longer address*. Some hotels go a step further and skip room 113 by going from room 111 to room 115 in the odd numbers. I've got more news—room 115 is room 113 *incorrectly numbered*.

Other high-rise hotels completely skip the thirteenth floor. So, if I'm on the fourteenth floor in a hotel with no thirteenth, and they put me in 1413 or 1415, I ain't checking in! If you are superstitious of 13, beware the wolf in sheep's clothing—number 15. I also like to be near a fire escape, and unless you've stayed in a hotel when a fire started, you may not even think of this. I have, and do.

If I ever get to Volume 13 in the *Grandpa Pike's* books, I'd like you to buy it, though. If you've survived twelve of these and haven't developed a nervous tic or a warped sense of reality, one more won't hurt you. Would I lie?

PARADING OUR DISABILITIES

IN THE SEVENTEENTH AND EIGHTEENTH CENTURIES, IF you had a hearing disability you could have a horn or air trumpet made to assist with your hearing. From that we have advanced in the twenty-first century to tiny powerful devices that fit inside the ear and go unseen by others.

Wheelchairs have become more and more sophisticated, and many are motorized and modified to allow the owner to participate in sports. They have become smaller, collapsible, more manoeuvrable, and lightweight.

Modern canes to assist walking all come with rubber tips to prevent sliding. Some are available with spiked tips to assist walking on ice and snow. Some will stand on their own. Most are lighter and more durable than earlier versions.

If you lose some of your natural teeth there are plates, partial plates, caps, and even individual replacement teeth available that screw directly into your jawbone.

Most modern aids to our disabilities tend to be hidden or designed so as not to attract attention. Dentures, for example, look as much like real teeth as possible. Hearing aids made to fit in the ear have no wires attached and simply "vanish," especially if the hair is worn over the ears.

That all makes sense. Why flaunt a disability? Nobody wants to order green or black dentures. With dentures, buying coloured ones would simply be stupid. Who needs to know you wear dentures?

Who would want an old-fashioned horn drawing attention to your hearing disability? (With hearing, though, perhaps it would be a benefit if there were some visual signal that you had a disability. Wouldn't others try to speak louder or more clearly?)

So, while most disability aids tend to hide or minimize your noticing them, there is one disability aid that stands out starkly as being purposely designed differently. Eyeglasses. They have become fashion, jewellery, and beauty aids. You can buy frames now in any colour of the rainbow—including rainbow-coloured. They are available with lights! What comes next—optional windshield wipers and turn signals?

Why do we take such effort to hide our deafness, for example, but shout to the world, "I can't see well"? We started centuries ago with rimless glasses and thin wire frames that did their best to hide the device, and then we went to contact lenses that are virtually undetectable. Now we move on to bright white plastic frames with red racing stripes?

You see more and more motorized carts or scooters at the malls and in downtown areas. Many of these people—though not all—have only one thing wrong with them. They are obese. Most of us with a sight disability would do more "looking," or "look harder," if it would improve our vision. Most would listen more intently, or turn the TV to a lower volume, if it would improve our hearing. Why, then, are we too lazy to walk a little bit, to improve our walking, so we won't end up riding in a cart?

DANDELIONS DUCK

EXCEPT FOR THEIR BRIGHT YELLOW FLOWER, AND THE spring's earliest greens which they provide to people in northern climes, the dandelion is a nuisance. The early settlers brought them here, unwittingly in some cases, by way of their parachute-like seeds that will land on and cling to anything. Other settlers brought plants for food, medicinal reasons, and probably to make dandelion wine. Did they thrive here? Come see my lawn!

The French called them *dent-de-lion* (lion's tooth) because of the jagged leaf. Here we call them pissabeds, and if you have these yellow "stains" on your otherwise pristine green lawn, you need not ask why. I'd like to get rid of the little bedwetters, but I don't want to use chemicals. Recently, because of the decline in honeybees, environmentalists are urging us to leave them unmowed—as they provide the first spring food for bees.

I have a friend who owns a GoPro camera, and he is willing to hook it up to the underside of my mower—he's working on how to keep the lens clean. Why do I want him to do this? I can't prove it, but I know that when you mow over them, dandelions duck! Don't believe me? Look behind you when you mow, and you'll see the clever little devils raise their yellow heads unscathed.

They have developed other strategies for survival, too. Some grow their long stems laterally, hiding in the grass until their heads are ready to open. Then they pop straight up at night while you're sleeping. Others, after a few generations in your lawn, put up only a very short stem.

You can groan and moan until the cows come home, but the only way to get rid of this dwarf variety is to bend over and pinch them off by hand.

For the longer ones, however, I've got to prove that they duck, and video evidence should verify my theory. Some of you won't believe me, and you'll say that it's the turbulence caused by the mower blades that causes them to blow over as the mower moves and thus escape decapitation.

You may say I'm confusing cause with effect. One of you will quote O. Henry from "The Ransom of Red Chief," where the little rascal asked, "Does the trees moving make the wind blow?" Unlike Red Chief, however, I intend to prove my theory and develop an automatic self-lowering blade that will put an end to my dandelion dilemma, or at least put a big dent in my jungle, my mighty jungle, where the damn *dent-de-lion* sleeps tonight.

— CHAPTER 5 —
GRANDPA'S BLACK PAGES

As any reader knows, life is not simply a series of rainbows and surprise birthday parties. There are storms—mild and massive—and surprises which you could have well done without. Here are a few of the storms that I've been through. I include them here as living proof that you can come out the other end unscathed. These things happen. They make you grow, and they make you appreciate the good times more.

THE OLD MAN

I GAZED AT MY FATHER LYING THERE ON THE HOSPITAL bed and couldn't help but think how small he looked. He was never a big man—maybe 5'2 or 5'3 tops. Now he had lost weight—shrunk. His coal-black hair was now white, his once ruddy face pale. He was a strong, robust man in my youth. He could put the fear of God in you, and I saw a few much bigger men back down from him. I had to look up at him until I was about seventeen and experienced a major growth spurt.

He was tiny now, unthreatening at age eighty-three, and he was dead. I had arrived in his hospital room moments after he passed away. My sisters and one of my brothers were there along with my father's second wife. (He had divorced my mother and later married a younger woman—just a few years older than me.) My siblings were waiting for the staff to wheel him out of the room. He had been expected to die and was unconscious when they arrived. I'd driven down from Moncton, New Brunswick, to the Highland View Regional Hospital in Amherst, Nova Scotia, as soon as I got the call.

My sister said he had been breathing slowly and they were watching and listening for each breath. Then, without warning, the next one never came. Nor would the answers to all the questions that I wished I had asked him. I knew the what, the when, and the how of much of his life, but there were some blank spaces. I never learned the why of many things.

Picture, if you can, a four-year-old boy, naked from the waist down, crying and trying to walk across the kitchen floor. It's a big, cold room—a kitchen table and chairs at one end, a wood cookstove at the other. A bare light bulb hangs on its cord from the centre of the ceiling. The floor is freezing cold. He can't read the words yet, but a plaster of Paris plaque on the wall reads CHRIST IS COMING SOON. He's crying because the coffee can tied around his waist, hanging below his genitals, keeps banging his legs as he moves.

That is the very first memory of my childhood. I was that little boy. In later years I wondered if the "tin can" thing had simply been a dream. I asked my sister, and she confirmed that it actually did happen. How long it went on, she could not recall.

It was my father's idea. Apparently he was tired of me wetting the bed and peeing in my day clothes. I don't know what device, if any, he employed at night to staunch the flow. I assume he did not tie a knot in my waterworks, if only because there wasn't enough there with which to work.

Physical Punishment is Abuse

WHEN YOU ARE VERY YOUNG YOU CRY BECAUSE OF THE pain. Later you cried because your pride was hurt. Having your pants pulled down and being beaten in front of your siblings is embarrassing and humiliating. When you get older, the humiliation turns to anger. The anger is magnified if the punishment is not proportional to the offence. The anger turns to silent rage and hatred should you be punished for something you didn't even do.

My crying was more from anger than hurt, and I promised myself that I would get even when I grew up. Most times you stopped crying, but if you didn't you'd really get the belt and be sent to bed without your supper. "Stop your whimpering or I'll give you something to cry about," said my father. (He always kept his word.) If this occurred at four in the afternoon, it made for a long night. You did what you were told to do, not so much because you learned your actions were wrong, but simply to avoid the punishment.

He was a lot easier on the girls, but if something got broken and no one would own up, he treated us all equally. He'd line us up, get us to bend over at the waist, and pull up our shirts or blouses. Then we would feel the full fury of his wrath as he went up and down the row with his leather belt, beating us on the back until he was tired or his anger dissipated. He used to call this the "bare back treatment."

You didn't flinch because you couldn't see the big black belt coming—bent over as you were, with your palms cupping your knees. You didn't hear it when it dropped as silently and swiftly as an eagle to its prey.

You felt the tiny breath of air on your back just before it struck, heard only the explosive *slap!* Like an echo, milliseconds later, came the sound of the second side of the doubled belt slapping against the first. Together they cut through your skin and into your flesh. You felt only the pain, again and again without warning, until . . . it stopped.

Next you heard your sibling subjected to the same pain, but you didn't dare move because he often came back down the line once or several times more.

God *hates* sin but *loves* the sinner, so said our father and a thousand other preachers as they tried to "save" the sinful. I now knew what anger looked and felt like, but what of love? What did love *feel* like? Was it soft and white like the underside of an angel's wing? What did it *sound* like?

Did it sound like the teacher's words of praise when you did well on the test? Was it like that warm feeling you got when opening up a Christmas present from a faraway aunt, or like the smile of a pretty girl at school? Is that what love felt like? I wondered but didn't know.

Not only could you hear and feel what anger was like, you could see how it looked when you got to a mirror and pulled up your shirt—but what of love? Maybe love was just being left alone. That's all I wanted. We didn't cry much—most of us, anyway. A child will cry only until the cry is beat out of him. I remember my sister crying a little. I believe it was because she really loved our father, and she was hurt, not just physically.

Why he would punish six kids when only one offended I don't know. I assume he thought that the one who offended by breaking a dish or the handle of a tool would own up rather than see their siblings suffer.

If it was a minor matter like tracking in dirt from outside, we'd all simply glance at the one who did it. They'd get yelled at, be told to clean it up, and it would be over. Sometimes it was hard to know which ones were minor offences, though, as that seemed to change with his mood. When anger darkened his face, we quickly went silent.

I learned early on that when being punished you were not to cry and just as quickly learned to despise him—like you would. When you are told not to cry, you are being denied the right to have emotions. I decided that if I could not cry I would not smile, either, my way, I suppose, of trying to exert some control. I went around showing no emotion at all. This continued well into adulthood.

Unless I was with really close friends, I went about my business looking very serious—so much so that in my twenties one of my co-workers started calling me Stone Face. That made me smile.

To my father, if you laughed too much, you were probably up to mischief. If you frowned, you were being moody or "crooked." Either way, it got his attention, and that could mean trouble. I tried to show no emotions except when alone reading or late at night daydreaming about getting big enough and strong enough to beat him up and then run away somewhere . . . anywhere.

My mother didn't have an easy life with my father, either. I remember the arguments and shouting late at night, after bedtime. I would cry myself to sleep, praying that he would not hurt her. It is a rare marriage where neither partner has raised their voice during an argument. I know he did much worse, though, when I was too young to intervene.

I clearly remember one incident that happened late one night. He would have thought the youngsters were all asleep. He dragged her down the hallway by the hair of her head. She was crying and screaming—begging for him to stop. All I could do as an eight-year-old was pretend to be asleep. My interference would have only made him angrier, with worse results for my mother.

I know there were other incidents during my childhood, but I don't remember any detail. I believe I've blocked them out. The sound of raised voices and arguments still echo.

I don't know for certain if he physically abused her later in life. If he did, I can only assume that the deeds were done when they were alone—a cowardly act at best, a criminal act at worst. Perhaps the kids knowing would have tarnished his carefully polished image. Maybe he "grew up," but I am more of the opinion that he learned how to hide his flaws, as many of us do.

Which demon is it that makes a man beat his own wife and children? Is it anger, frustration, or a learned response from having been beaten himself—and having seen *his own* mother beaten? Still, had he only taken me aside later and told me he was sorry, just once, I could have forgiven him. If he was going to beat someone, however, I was satisfied that it was me and not my mother.

When I heard his raised voice late at night coming from my parents' bedroom, I would roll over on my other side to make it stop. It stopped. I don't remember at what age I came to realize that it stopped when I turned over because I was nearly deaf in my left ear. I know—and I am truly not trying to make light of it here—but in "turning a deaf ear" and pretending I was asleep, it probably made it easier on Mom.

I promised myself early on that if I ever had a wife or kids, I would never strike them. I've never struck a woman. I only ever did it once—to a tiny girl—a couple of slaps on the bum of my four-year-old daughter when she ran down our driveway toward the busy roadway. I was angry because she had frightened me. She cried. I felt ashamed afterwards. I never sensed shame or regret from my father.

When I hear a woman crying, it rips the heart out of me. No matter how a woman gets "in my face," no matter what she calls me, no matter how she might belittle me, I will never strike a woman. Never.

I can still hear my mother crying.

THE HEAVIEST LOAD

I WAS SITTING IN A BIG COUNTRY AND WESTERN SHOW BAR in Dartmouth one night, in the mid-'70s, listening to my friend Wally Ganyon and his band, Brother Love. I was alone, and a young musician from Newfoundland came over and asked if he could sit with me. I'd never met him, but I had seen his picture. I knew he was A. Frank Willis.

Frank was on his way across the country, trying to get his name better known outside of Newfoundland. He came over to me because he saw me with the band and mistook me for their manager. He was looking for gigs and venues anywhere in the Maritimes on his journey west. Like all musicians I have known, he did not talk when others were performing, only between songs. I told him to stay until break and meet Wally.

Wally and his band were well-established in the Maritimes area

 and always drew a crowd. Frank stayed, and Wally spent that whole break and the next one writing down names of people he could stay with, bars where he could play, and phone numbers. It just seemed natural between the two of them—and A. Frank knew places where Wally could play and stay in Newfoundland. It impressed me,

though, that musicians would go out of their way to help and to support another—who might later become a competitor.

In business, this attitude was foreign to me. In a sports analogy, it would be like one challenger for a boxing title showing another all his moves and tricks. Musicians, however, are different. While some music *fans* will only listen to one genre, *musicians* tend to support all other musicians and appreciate any form. I'll never forget how those two guys bonded in minutes as if they had known each other their whole lives. That's the way it was between Wally and me, too. I first met him in 1975, shortly after he left the RCMP to make a career in country music.

When he left the force, his marriage came apart and he was divorced from his wife and estranged from his two daughters. Wally and I spent time together when he wasn't working. If I was in a town where he was performing, I'd spend the evening at the venue.

We became close. Close as brothers. He stayed at my farm in Yarmouth County when he played that area. Later, he moved to Moncton, and I moved there as well. He began appearing fairly regularly on a country music TV show out of Halifax and recorded a couple of singles in a studio. One, "Celia," did quite well and got considerable airplay—across the country. Then Wally married a widow with three daughters.

Wally wanted to settle down in Albert County, New Brunswick, as soon as he got better established. To that end, he decided, like A. Frank, to get his name better known outside his own region. In 1980, at age thirty-two, he moved with his wife and the girls to Alberta. He said he'd be back in two years. We phoned each other many times, and every once in a while I'd get a letter or a postcard signed, "Your brother Wally."

Wally worked as a single act out west and recorded an album called *Kitchen Pickin'*. Two years later, he bought an old school bus, converted it to a touring vehicle, and prepared to move the family back to New Brunswick. Late that night, with all the family asleep and Wally still driving, he saw a truck—broken down.

Without waking the family, he moved his bus to a position facing the truck where they could use the bus's headlights to work under the truck's hood. Moments later, Wally's wife, Kathy, woke up to the sensation of a sudden jolt, the sound of a crash, and then silence. She saw that Wally was not in the driver's seat and noticed the four-way flashers were on.

She thought he must have pulled over to help at an accident. She saw nothing outside but dark. Now fully awake and puzzled, she went outside to look. She called his name, and there was no answer. Then she noticed his legs sticking out from under the bus. She looked under the bus, but the rest of him wasn't there.

A couple of drunks had driven a car into the rear of the bus—on the shoulder—thinking they were in a driving lane. The bus had jolted forward and trapped Wally between the bus and the pickup truck, and he fell in pieces to the ground. The pickup driver panicked and left—but was later found. The drunks in the car were either knocked out or they passed out on impact.

Late that morning I got a phone call, and that night I flew to Winnipeg, then got a rental and drove to Petersfield, Manitoba, Wally's birthplace, for the funeral. In the two days before the funeral, his friends all congregated at the one motel in town. The rooms ran out quickly, and some of us slept in cars, on the floor of the hallway, and in sleeping bags outside. They were from every province, and there were Aboriginals, Metis, French, English and "other—or as Wally used to say, "I'm half French and half crazy."

Kathy told me later, "I don't mind telling you, I was a tad nervous when I woke up this morning to see a large Aboriginal guy sitting at the foot of my bed." "Don't worry," he whispered, "Wally was my best friend when we were kids. We used to play cowboys and Indians together. Wally always wanted to be the Indian, so I was the cowboy." He smiled and talked in a soft voice about Wally until, exhausted, she fell asleep again.

It was a beautiful sunny day and the church was full, then they opened up the doors so that those in the hallway could hear, and finally the outside doors for the crowd who couldn't even get in. There were Mounties, musicians, businessmen and buddies, school chums, fans, teachers, and preachers. They walked up or drove up in battered pickups and brand new Lincolns. The cross-section of people there said a lot about the kind of person he was. Six of us carried this dear friend out of the church to his final resting place. It was the heaviest load I've ever had to bear.

What I remember most about Wally was his sense of humour. I can still picture him walking down the streets in Yarmouth wearing a T-shirt, a big cowboy hat, cowboy boots, and shorts! Once, when he was playing at the Grand Hotel in Yarmouth, we were on our way up the elevator to his changing room.

An elderly couple with a strong Bostonian accent got on. "Is the orchestra here any good?" the old man asked. "Naw," said Wally, "they are pretty poor. The shits—I don't think you'd like them at all."

They were silent for a moment, and then the lady turned to Wally. "You're . . . you're the singer," she announced with a big smile. "I saw your picture on the poster."

"You got me!" Wally laughed, giving her a hug that brought a smile to her husband's face as well. "We might be a bit loud, though. It's hard to please everyone."

"Oh, that's okay, sir," she assured him as they got off at their floor." "It's not *easy* being a star."

They did show up later, loved the music and Wally's bantering on stage, and danced until the show was over. Wally had fun with her line later, and any time something would go wrong, on stage or off, he'd sigh, shake his head, and say, "It's not *easy* being a star."

He was thirty-four when he died, and it's been thirty-seven years since. I've never forgotten his laugh. I'll always treasure his friendship. I've buried both my parents, a sister and a brother, but no death has affected me as profoundly as Wally's. I hope I'll never have to carry that heavy a load again.

FOR JIM

MY OLD FRIEND LAY FLAT ON HIS BACK IN THE HOS-pital bed, tubes coming out of his arm and nose. Frail and un-conscious, he was not expected to live this long. I had rushed to the hospital to see him when I heard. His wife staggered to her feet as I arrived. At his side for almost twenty-four hours, she was exhausted. I urged her to go get something to eat and I would stay with him until she returned. She reluctantly agreed.

As I sat and stared, I began thinking about what Jim was like when we worked together years ago—loyal, progressive, visionary. We worked well as a team trying to resurrect a company caught in a time warp. Not just at work, but countless evenings driving out over the road, and in hotels, we talked well into the night. I knew his wife, but we had only met at a couple of company functions. Jim and I didn't discuss personal matters. We talked almost exclusively about business. We were on a mission.

Serious about his work but carefree and lighthearted about all else, he could always think of something funny or ironic to say even in the most dire of circumstances. Now things were deadly serious, and I wished I could hear his voice. Then, as God is my witness, his eyes opened. He wet his lips, and I heard him say, "Life's a bitch . . . and then you die."

I smiled but said nothing as he stared steadily at the ceiling. Then he blinked, and a tear rolled out of the corner of his eye. He started speaking, laboriously at first, in snippets, seemingly unaware that I was there. Expressing thoughts as if he were talking to a priest or minister. I should have called a nurse, but I didn't. I was compelled to listen.

"There's another woman. I love her . . . small . . . a slip of a woman . . . younger than me . . . the way she talks . . . that lilt in her voice . . . the way she carries herself. Her nose, her chin. Her eyes could drown you. Afraid to look into them for long . . . fear I will blurt out, 'I love you.' Ruin things for everyone. We can't be together . . . married . . . to someone else . . . long to be near her . . . to hear that voice. I could die in peace . . . close enough to hear her heart beat . . . feel her breathing on my skin . . . feel her warmth . . . just to hold her."

He blinked again, and the tears fell freely. He turned his head to look at me, as if he had known all along that I was there. Then he commenced to whisper again, laboriously, "A real lady . . . nice dresser . . . looks great in black . . . long hair . . . wears earrings . . . ears turn out a little . . . at the top . . . love that . . . I could chew the ears right off her!" He smiled, and his words came slower now, with more effort. "Gentle . . . kind . . . soft as a kitten . . . don't know how she feels . . . but . . . I love her."

His words were a shock to me. All those nights that we spent in hotel bars having a cold one and strategizing for our next meetings, he showed no interest in other women. He was not a skirt chaser. I have no idea what his relationship with his wife was like, but I s'pose it must be some kind of hell to be "tied" to one woman and be deeply in love with another.

I was hoping that his wife would return and at the same time praying that she wouldn't until he was finished talking. "Do you want me to tell this woman?" I asked.

"No," he whispered. "I hoped we could be together . . . somehow . . . some way . . . if I knew that she loved me . . . you could tell her." He said a few more words, which I'll tell you later.

Still, I had no idea who this woman was. Then, suddenly, his head slumped. He stopped breathing, and the monitor by the bed began making a beeping sound. He was gone.

I jumped up to alert staff at the nurses' station, but almost simultaneously two nurses showed up and worked frantically on him. Next, a doctor arrived. Then his wife came back, and I was asked to leave. I went down to the waiting area outside intensive care, pondering his words. Clearly he wanted me to know his secret. It was nearly 2:00 a.m., and I was the only one there. I waited and waited for his wife or a nurse to come and confirm that he had passed over.

Finally, a small slip of a woman, dressed in black, walked in the front door. With her long hair pulled back into a ponytail, I noticed her earrings and that her ears turned out a little at the top. I'd met this lady and seen her many times at social gatherings around town. I'd never noticed her ears before. Instantly I knew that she was the woman whom Jim had described. Absolutely sure. I smiled, thinking about his words as she acknowledged me and came over to sit down.

"He's gone," I told her. "Not officially, but I'm quite sure he's gone."

With that, she burst into tears, and I tried to comfort her.

"He was a special friend," she told me quietly.

"He talked about you. He loved you," I said. "I asked him if he wanted me to tell you. He said, 'No, but if I knew that she loved me, you could.' But I guess it's okay to tell you now. He didn't want to hurt you, if you didn't feel the same way." She wept softly.

I told her all the kind and wonderful things he had said about her. And I had to tell her those last few words he said—words that I knew would convince her that he had loved her—that this was Jim talking and not me making up words of consolation. These were Jim's last words:

"Even if we were single . . . don't know if I could tell her . . . out of respect . . . have to have a lot of respect for a woman . . . to tell her I love her . . . how could I respect a woman . . . even the most wonderful one that God ever gave breath . . . if she was stunned enough . . . to love a raggedy-arsed guy like me?'"

"That's Jim," she laughed through her tears. "That's Jim, all right." I promised the lady that I would never tell his wife what I knew. She got up to leave as soon as the nurse arrived to tell me that Jim was indeed gone. The nurse said that his wife wanted me to come in. I saw the lady to her car and went back in to Jim's bedside to console his wife. I missed the funeral, as I had to be out of town on business. Shortly after, I was transferred to another province. I haven't seen either woman since.

So, Jim, I don't know for certain if she loved you. She didn't really say. Perhaps she couldn't . . . but I saw her cry, and I believe that I saw love in her eyes. I hope that is of some comfort to you.

As I drove home from the hospital through that dark early morning, Jim, I turned the radio on to news of break-ins, a murder, a missing child, and a bad moose-vehicle collision. No good news.

I clicked the radio's SEEK button, and it started playing a song by The Eagles from their first album—the classic "Peaceful Easy Feeling." A song you loved, back in the day, and would crank the radio up to bust when it came on during our drives. *I like the way your sparkling earrings lay . . .*

I know now, Jim, that she was likely the woman of whom you were thinking on those long rides. I had to tell her. Hope you're not angry. And when I pulled into my driveway, I sat and listened until the very end of the song. Then the DJ said, "I *looove* that song! An anonymous female caller sent in that request—just for you, Jim."

FOR *CHRIST'S* SAKE!

WHILE I WAS RECORDING MY SECOND CD FOR THE Children's Wish Foundation in Newfoundland and Labrador, my sister Hazel was on her deathbed in Nova Scotia. That album, entitled *For* Christ's *Sake!*, was gospel. We recorded it on the Victoria Day weekend in May 2009. The session at Hockey Gale's studio in the Codroy Valley of Newfoundland had been planned for some time.

I talked to my family, and they all told me not to cancel, as Hazel was in a coma and it was impossible to tell if or when her condition might improve or worsen. They would contact me, and I could rush over to Nova Scotia if necessary. There was nothing I could do, so I decided to stay and record.

In a conversation some years earlier, Hazel had told me that one of her favourite Gospel songs was "Shall We Gather at the River." I wanted to include it in this CD, and we did.

It was a tough weekend, and here, in part, are the liner notes I wrote some weeks later.

> My sister Hazel passed away at age sixty-six, on May 20, 2009. She didn't get a whole lot of breaks in life—although she was blessed with three children she loved dearly. She married young.

One Sunday morning, while at church with her kids, their house and all possessions went up in smoke and flames. Later, there was a marriage breakdown and she was plagued with medical issues. Despite that, she worked—harder than she should have.

Finally, in the last couple of years, she got a house paid off and bought her first decent vehicle. It was time to retire and put the drudgery behind her. She went into the hospital for a knee operation to relieve the constant pain.

She came through fine, but a blood clot the next day put her at Heaven's gate, and she crossed over a few days later. Hockey will attest that it took all I had, emotionally, to record this song.

Our family was old-school, and when we were kids there was not much talk of love or showing of affection. I now find it tragic, but in the sixty-five years I knew her, I didn't tell her once that I loved her . . . not even once!

I got an update daily from my wife, Katie, and Hazel's condition was unchanged the first day. The next morning, I drove to Port aux Basques for a Tim Hortons. All the way out and back again, I was struck with the unfairness of it all. She had struggled for everything she got in life. It had come easy for me. I have had all that I needed, as much as I wanted, and more than I deserved. I decided to make an offer to God.

I stopped at Precious Blood Roman Catholic Church and tried to get inside. It was locked. I drove on across the valley, down near the lighthouse, to Holy Trinity Anglican Church. It too was locked, so I walked around to the back and knelt there on the steps. I asked God if He would take me in her place. Give her a chance for a few good years.

Later that day, as I was in the studio, there came a call from Katie. It looked like there might be improvement. Hazel, she was told, was now reacting to stimuli! Believing God may have accepted my plea,

I wrote a note in the ledger I was keeping for the session. The exact words escape me now but are in my files somewhere.

It said something like, "If I die and you read this, don't feel bad. It was okay with me." I signed my name and dated it. She did not get better, though. The next day, the news was negative again. Finally, she was brain-dead, and they pulled the plug.

Maybe for just a moment God considered my offer. Or maybe it was just a coincidence.

Perhaps there is no God. No matter how much the fanatics argue for and against, no one alive knows for sure. In any event, I was ready to go. The final two lines of my liner notes about "Shall We Gather" and Hazel read like this:

As God Almighty is my witness, so let the record show,
That I have always loved you—I just failed to tell you so.

Hazel Shirley Pike

BAMBI

I HAVE A TATTOO HIGH ON MY RIGHT SHOULDER THAT few have ever seen. There's a bit of scrollwork and a heart with the word "Bambi" inside that heart. She has always stayed there. I had it done in New Orleans back in the early 1970s. I see it every morning when I have my shower and again at night when I prepare for bed . . . and I remember. It's faded now. I am one of the very few who can read it and tell you what it says—since I don't plan to get naked with you! But now, anyone who reads this will know.

I met her back when I was working in the grocery business. At the supermarket, all full-time staff had their own section to manage. The health and beauty aids department was hers. My section was nearby. She was tall and slim, blonde, blue-eyed, and quite pretty. She had those big trusting eyes and a little turned-up nose, and I nicknamed her Bambi.

Our relationship started with joking around. She seemed to find me funny. She started to open up a bit when I asked her about herself. She was divorced, and it sounded like she had not had a good marriage. I guess I wanted to prove to her that men are not all the same, and in the process I fell for her. We started dating and within months were talking marriage.

Her parents didn't like me—especially her mother. The first time

Bambi took me home, her mother asked would I like a drink. I told her that a beer would be great. "We don't keep alcohol in this house," she announced without a smile. I had a coffee, but on future occasions she continued to ask me, "Would you like a drink?" with a smirk on her face.

That Christmas her mother gave me a present. Imagine the look of shock on my face when I unwrapped an electric razor—since I wore a beard at the time! "It will be so easy to shave now," she said. The inference being that I was too lazy to do it with a safety razor.

We stayed together the next year, and by mid-year we decided to set a marriage date. At the same time I started thinking about a career change. I had always wanted to leave retail and get into outside sales. Now was the time to get started.

In the fall I applied for a position with a major soft drink company which was seeking someone to call on the head offices of their key accounts. I got an interview and the job.

I was walking on air when I gave my notice, and when I was asked why I was leaving, I was so proud of the new job, I told my manager. About a week later, as I was working out my two-week notice period, I received a call from the soft drink company's personnel department. "We've done some reorganizing, sales are down, and we have decided *not* to fill the position we offered you." I was devastated—as it was a big increase in income, and a company vehicle went with the job.

Another employee told me, in confidence, that my manager had called the soft drink company, complaining about them raiding his staff. They promised to reconsider. I suppose he thought if I didn't get that job, I would come back to him begging to be kept on. Instead, I didn't show up for work the next day. I've never seen him since.

This was in October, and we had planned to be married December 1. Here I was without a job, and Bambi's mother drove me crazy asking what was I going to do, did I have a job yet? Bambi seemed all right with it, so we went ahead and rented an apartment and bought some furniture. Meanwhile, I was looking for work and applying for any outside sales positions that came up.

On December 1, we drove to Toronto, went to the Justice of the Peace at city hall, and were married. On December 2, I left the family I was boarding with and relocated all my worldly goods to the new apartment. Then we moved Bambi's possessions in as well.

Her mother called every night. I could tell by Bambi's responses that the old girl was asking, "Did *he* go looking for work today?" and "What will you do if *he* doesn't get a job?"

It was putting a strain on our marriage. I knew I would find something. I could get a job in the food business easily if I couldn't find something in outside sales.

As the middle of December approached, however, I could feel Bambi pulling away from me. She got quiet and then quieter, and her mother continued to phone. On December 19, I got a call from Ted Kaiser of Crest Hardware. We talked on the phone for about an hour. He wanted to interview me, in person, on the twenty-first, for a position selling to hardware stores. That appointment was later rescheduled to December 23—a Sunday—as Ted was unable to keep the first meeting but wanted someone in place for the first of the year. I got the job!

I rushed home to tell Bambi the good news, bounding up the stairs to our apartment two at a time. I opened the door and burst in. For a moment I thought I had the wrong apartment—as this one was empty! The furniture was gone; even the curtains were down. The closets were empty, and the only place to sit was on the toilet. I sat and I broke down. Clearly her family had moved her out during the three hours I had been gone.

I found my clothes—minus the coat hangers—on the floor of the hall closet, along with my other personal items. I saw a few garbage bags under the kitchen sink and carried away what was left of my life in them. Then I drove over to my friend's—Peter the mailman. We drank more than a few beers. The next thing I remember, it was Boxing Day, and on December 27 or 28 I moved back to the Connells', where I had previously boarded.

So, that was my first marriage—twenty-three days!

We got legally separated through lawyers by mail—without having to see each other—and in like manner subsequently divorced. I went on to a long career in sales and marketing, remarried, and had a child.

It was years later before I saw Bambi again. We spent quite a few hours together that evening, talking. She told me that she had panicked and wished that it hadn't been so. It was over, though, and we both knew it. Her mother is now dead and buried.

I know it is wrong to disrespect the dead, but I can't help but wonder whether the undertaker was skilled enough to be able to remove the smile from her face. Bet she'd have removed Bambi from my heart, too—if she could. She failed at that.

The Girl with the Clear Blue Eyes

IT WAS QUITE A WHILE AFTER MY FIRST WIFE, BAMBI, LEFT that I started dating again. About a year later, I met a girl who was known to her friends as Gabby. I was in Burlington, Ontario, at a bar called the Ponderosa, listening to a musician friend, Gord Elston, who was performing there. I wasn't interested in girls that night—just there for the beer and music.

A group of about eight to ten women in their twenties and most of them attractive walked in. They had just gotten out of a Tupperware or some such party. Gabby smiled at me as I walked past to the men's room. I was surprised that this blue-eyed, dark-haired beauty even noticed me, but I smiled back and nodded.

When I got back from the washroom, I casually glanced across the room—not to be too obvious—to see if I could see her again. My line of vision was blocked by another lady in the group—the one who sat beside Gabby—who was now coming over to ask me to dance. She wasn't terribly attractive. I know how difficult it is to go over and ask someone to dance—with all eyes on you—and how embarrassing it is to have to walk back to your table alone. I couldn't do that to her, even though I wasn't really into dancing that night. I'm glad that we danced.

Gord was now singing "Great Balls of Fire," and on the crowded dance floor this lady and I were directly in front of him. Gord had this thing where in the last line of the song he would change the words—and look at the nearest person to gauge the reaction.

My partner was looking right up at him, and you should have seen the look on her face as he jumped off his stool and sang, "Goodness, gracious—my *balls are on fire!*"

On the way back to her table she said, "My friend Gabby wants to meet you." I hoped it would be the girl who smiled at me. It was. I took Gabby home that night, and we started dating. She was fun and happy and carefree and full of life—most days. Separated, she had her own small apartment in Hamilton. Her two preteen sons stayed over some weekends with her but lived with their father in a nearby town. Gabby didn't work. She had been a full-time mother and homemaker.

After we went out a few times, I started staying over some nights, and other times she would come over to my place. We talked about living together, but I didn't want to do that until my divorce was final. Truthfully, I wanted to be absolutely sure we were compatible and that I could deal with two kids and more, perhaps, if we eventually married.

As I hinted above, she wasn't always carefree and happy. Sometimes she was moody and down in the dumps. I chalked it up to how she was living—alone and away from her kids. One night I noticed a pill bottle on her dresser. I asked her about it, and she told me that she was being treated for depression—and admitted that this was why she was living near the hospital and not working.

She began to tell me her fears. She said how her husband was out to get her, and how she knew he had guns and knives hidden in the walls, and was going to try to kill her. She had taken the drywall off in places but was unable to locate the weapons.

I started to panic as she confided more and more of her fears. I didn't understand depression—who did in those days? Depressed people were either simply "feeling sorry for themselves" or "crazy." Sometimes she was perfect—loving and kind. Other times she would get dark and try to convince me that her fears were real. What was I getting myself into? I couldn't let go because I cared about her.

One Friday, we went to visit the Connells—my "second family"—and stayed overnight. Saturday morning, as we were sitting around talking with Jim, she went to the bathroom for what seemed like an inordinate length of time. We were downstairs in the rec room, so I decided to go upstairs to see if anything was wrong. When I knocked on the door, she started screaming and shouting at me. The door was locked, so I ran downstairs to ask Jim if I should break it open.

As I was asking this, all in a panic, we heard a door slam. Running upstairs, we discovered the bathroom door open, razor blades on the floor, and blood everywhere. Gabby was gone. We followed her trail to the front door and went outside to look. Jim wanted to call the police or an ambulance—I wanted to find her first.

Jim checked the yard and the neighbouring backyard, and I got in my car and drove the short distance up the street to the mall. I saw her crouched down by a storage shed. She didn't see me, so I hurried back and we called the police. The police sent an ambulance, which arrived along with an unmarked car. She went quietly with the police, and they escorted her to the ambulance.

The police knew her, and she was known to the ambulance drivers, as this had happened before. They took her to the hospital where she was being treated. Gabby was there for about three weeks, if memory serves. This would have been the perfect time to "disappear," but I couldn't do that. I went to see her, but they were allowing only her husband and kids to visit. I went to see her husband to find out how she was doing. He was a real gentleman, given the circumstance that I was seeing his wife—whom he still loved.

He told me about her long history of mental illness and treatment. She was fine if she stayed on her medications, but she would not. I decided that now it was time to bow out, as I could tell he was no monster and had her best interests at heart. I wanted the kids to forget about me, too. I quit answering the phone, and when she was released from hospital, I did not call.

One night, a quiet knock came at my door. It was the happy Gabby, and she had just gotten back in town from a long weekend with some friends. She wanted to go out and get something to eat and to talk. We went.

I told her that she should go back with her husband and sons—who loved her. She wanted no part of it. She said she wanted to stay the night with me. I caved, and we went back to my place. It was now getting late, and I had to work in the morning and needed to get to sleep. She wanted to talk all night. We did talk until about 2:00 a.m. and had a few beers.

Eventually, I told her I was going to bed. She got angry and said she would walk home. I convinced her to stay, as it was not a safe neighbourhood for a woman to be walking late at night.

Finally, she went to bed and was sleeping, so I took a pillow, a blanket, and my alarm clock and went to sleep on the couch in the living room. I didn't want to risk waking her.

After my alarm sounded, I got up, got ready for work, and then slipped in beside her on the bed. I wanted to tell her I was leaving and she could stay as long as she wanted. She was lying on her side, facing the wall. I poked her, but she didn't flinch. Thinking she was just pretending to be asleep, I rolled her on her back. Her beautiful, clear blue eyes were open, but she was dead—and cold.

I grabbed the phone in panic and called the police. When I went into the kitchen, I saw the spilled pills and empty bottles on the countertop and knew what she had done. I was in shock. The police were wonderful. Once again, they knew her, and they called her husband. He met them at the station, or perhaps it was the morgue, to identify her.

The next few days were a blur. The last few words we had were in anger. I never got to tell her that I was sorry, nor she me, as we had always done before. I don't remember the chronology of events for the next few days. I believe it was Jim Connell or his dad who went back to my apartment and cleaned it up, moving all my belongings to their house. I never went back to that apartment and have never driven down that street since.

After the autopsy and before the funeral, the police told me that Gabby died of a brain hemorrhage, likely triggered as an effect of the pills. I sent flowers, and I went to her funeral. Again, her husband was gracious and kind, even though he felt as badly, I'm sure, and more than likely worse than me. I've never quite gotten over the feeling, though, that I am somehow responsible.

At the funeral, a girlfriend of Gabby's approached me and asked if she could have a ring and necklace which I had given her. The necklace had a cluster of rubies on a gold chain. The matching ring had five or six rubies surrounding a larger one in the centre. Emotional, and with little time to consider it, I said yes.

Later, I regretted letting the undertaker remove the ring and necklace that she loved so much before burying her. I wished I hadn't done it.

In the story "Bambi," I told you about the tattoo on my right shoulder. On my left is another—for Gabby. It was done in Tampico, Mexico. So, naturally, I see her name and think of her often. Within a few months of her passing, I left Ontario and went back to Nova Scotia to live. It took many years before I stopped seeing the girl with the clear blue eyes every time I closed mine.

— CHAPTER 6 —
RANTING AND ROARING

Some experiences frustrate you—make you angry or sad. Others make you laugh. A few just take all the good out of you, leaving you fit to be tied. Whichever way you react, the experience was worth going through because you have grown and are stronger for it. So it is with the following stories. At the end you may laugh or cry—sometimes in the same story—if I did my job right.

CAMPING

I DON'T UNDERSTAND THE ATTRACTION OF CAMPING, and I never will. Why in the name of common sense would one leave a perfectly good home—loaded with all the conveniences—and go out into the wilderness and pretend to be a nomad or a refugee? There'll be no fridge or stove, running water, or even a toilet! It will rain the whole time you are there, and the wildlife and insects will battle each other to get into the tent and gnaw on your flesh.

You won't be able to keep a fire going outside because of the rain. No rain in the forecast? Doesn't matter, trust me, it *will rain*. The only thing you can do inside is read—if you open the flap for enough light to do so, you'll either get wet or be eaten alive by swarms of winged tormenters—the devil's own air force.

As brave as you are, you will hear noises at night that you never heard before—even in the inner city. Blood-curdling sounds that will remind you of the way "Indians" communicated with each other, just before the big ambush and massacre, in an old western movie. You'll jump to your feet, but you are taller than the tent, and it will collapse around you. Then you'll trip, fall, and roll downhill into the lake. The tent will float away, taking with it your food, books, and fishing supplies. If luck fails you, you'll make it back to shore.

You'll sit with your back to a tree all night, cold, hungry, and unable to sleep as you listen to the serenade of unseen predators. At dim light of dawn you can see your car, parked off in the distance, and you get to it safely.

You've lost your keys—probably in the lake—so you break a window with a rock, sending a glittering shower of glass across the whole interior—but you get inside.

Exhausted, you lie down on the back seat. You notice a can of something under the front seat that must have rolled out from a grocery bag. It has a pull tab, so you open it, and you eat it with your fingers. Then you pass out.

When you start to regain consciousness, it is high noon, the sun is out, and it is stifling hot in the car. Mosquitoes, blackflies, and all their cousins are chewing on your corpse—their access made easier by the broken window, their job simplified by your multiple bleeding cuts from broken glass. Then you become aware of a rotten smell, but you move gingerly as you fear a skunk has sought refuge with you. Finally, you realize it is from the can of cold baked beans you ate. Now you've even become your own worst enemy.

You get out of the car, even though it is pouring rain again. You sit there, your back against the front tire, and cry—a broken man. Eventually your wife drives up. She was too smart to believe all the camping hype and wouldn't participate in your little experiment. She simply stopped by to see how your wilderness weekend was going. Now she listens to your story, trying not to laugh too hard, as she hauls your sorry arse home.

So You Want a Child, Eh?

A S JOAN RIVERS, REST HER SOUL, USED TO SAY, CAN WE talk? No, let's not talk about a baby's first Christmas, their first day at school, the day they join Brownies, or the first time they skin a knee and you kiss it and make it better. This is not about their first goal scored in hockey, their graduation, their wedding, or anything like that. You will remember all of those events for the rest of your life, though.

I want to talk about the *lifetime commitment*. They'll make you proud, and they'll disappoint you. They'll bring you joy, and they'll bring you pain. You will love them but at times not like them. When they reach twelve or thirteen and tell you, even once, that they don't love you anymore, it will break your heart.

When they create a special gift for your birthday, your spirit will soar. When you let them make their own important decision for the first time, and they choose wrong, your heart will ache. You are on a roller coaster from which you cannot escape. You will not even want to, but you are frightened to death on most of the ride.

Once you have a child, that child will be the first thought of your day and the last one at night—forever. You and your spouse will become secondary. No matter what you have to deal with, their needs will be foremost. May god forbid that you lose a child before your own time comes. I cannot even imagine the pain that you would go through.

Once your child has their education and moves away from home, your worries will not cease. Their health, their financial situation, their safety, their relationships will concern you. When anything goes wrong in their life, you will share in the sorrow and the pain that is theirs.

You wish you could take their place. If you could assume their load of worries, you would gladly take them on your own back. While you can't take their place, you will load those worries on your shoulders anyway, on top of your own. The weight of your own worries will seem insignificant as you concentrate on theirs. I'm still alive, so I don't know for certain, but I suspect that your dying thoughts and worries will be of them or for them.

They'll make you laugh out loud, and they'll make you cry softly at night—into your pillow, so they don't hear.

I have one child, and I would not have another for a million dollars, and I would not trade the one I have for all the money that Trump thinks he has. It's your decision to make. Make the right one. I did.

GARDENING

DON'T DO IT!

If you're really bored and need something to do with your summers, take up mountain climbing, or skydiving, or water skiing in shark-infested waters—anything would be less risky for your health and sanity than gardening. I've gardened all my life, and I couldn't survive for one winter on all that I've grown in that time. Lean back and let me tell you about the heartaches.

Depending on where you live, worms or raccoons will kill your corn, and cutworms chomp the stems off your transplants. Potato bugs will infest your spuds. Moths and caterpillars will chew your cabbage. Starlings will steal your strawberries, and little green worms the exact same colour as your broccoli will hide in the heads and only come out when you cook them.

Slugs will eat anything. Snails aren't cute. They're just slugs that live in mobile homes.

Rabbits and groundhogs will grab anything green. Robins will eat your earthworms, and deer and moose will chew all the new growth from your ornamental trees and shrubs. Late frost will kill your first planting, early frost your last one. You'll get drought when you need water and monsoons when you need dry. It will make you question your faith in God, quit going to church, and start voting NDP.

Little blackflies (no-see-ums) will fly up your nose and into your cranium and bite, horseflies (they call them stouts here) will pitch in the exact middle of your back—where you cannot reach—and stab you.

If you try to pull a weed away from anything with a blossom, the bees will sting you. Swarms of mosquitoes (nippers) the size of Sea King helicopters will darken the sky if there is any hint of rain.

But it won't rain—especially if you desperately need it. It'll hail—stones the size of softballs with ragged edges that'll tear the leaves off everything except the zucchini. Then armies of ants will march in to cut up the shredded leaves and carry them off to their hills.

Now with all your plants dead, and the hail over, the sun will come out and nature's air force of stouts, nippers, and no-see-ums will descend in wave after wave and attack all their favourite parts of your body. Finally, you'll go stark raving mad, tear off all your clothing, and run naked and screaming into the nearest woods.

No—don't do it! Buy a little mini-fridge for the screened-in veranda and a small portable TV to watch ball games. Fill the fridge with a big box of beer and sit there and drink it until the urge for gardening passes.

A WALK THROUGH A
PLACENTIA GRAVEYARD

I'LL TELL YOU LATER WHY I CAME HERE, BUT PLEASE JOIN me in the walk first.

It is, surprisingly, a cheerful place. Flowers, statues of angels, nicely painted rails, or low cement walls around the family plots—not unlike the picket fence around a home place. Some graves have white granite chips, others chipped brick, still others have shrubs and flowers. Everything is laid out in streets and side streets where the dead reside.

Many are still in family groupings, brothers, sisters, children, close together just as many of them lived, here in Placentia. It's "The Other Side," though, and whether or not you believe in life after death, this is where we will leave them. This is where they are still—the remains of their bodies, at least, and our memories.

The history of this town goes back over 350 years. The oldest gravestone still existing dates back to 1709, but even before that time this community was honouring its dead. The settlers, both French and English, were people of faith.

Like such people everywhere, they erected monuments to memorialize in perpetuity those who passed through—the revered, the rogues, the rich, and the ragged. From infants to centenarians, they celebrated each life, as we all should. Their age or their station in life immaterial. If their lives mattered to one, they should matter to all.

The pioneers started this cemetery at the very peak of the highest hill, a long time ago—each resident with a wonderful view of the ocean. They can't see, of course. We know that, but we like to believe that our loved ones' spirits can come back and look out over their loved and familiar landscape.

Slowly, the graveyard has crept down the hill, and now the newer residents can no longer see the ocean for the trees. Later the trees will be gone to make room for more people, and then all will again have a view of the sea.

Some folks fear going to graveyards, and I suspect it is because they fear death. I'm sure I could sleep in one, if necessary. The worst that is likely to happen is that it will rain or snow or a stray dog will pee on your pant leg. You are as safe as or safer in a graveyard than almost any other place on earth.

As I walk through the graveyard this morning in this small Newfoundland community, I am taking particular note of that which is engraved on the tombstones. Your gravestone is really your obituary.

We made the earlier stones of slate or sandstone and later granite. Stone is the hardest natural substance that will last. We want our descendants, and even complete strangers like me, here today, to know that the departed was loved, was special to those left behind.

You want to include as much pertinent information as possible but are severely restricted by space. When you read a gravestone, you need to see more than just the words, because everything else about it can tell you almost as much.

If there are Crosses, they were religious people, and most likely considered themselves Christian—or at least their family did. A Star of David—Jewish; a Crescent—Muslim.

A large headstone or monument means the family was well-to-do—a smaller one, of more modest means.

A rose or a daisy indicates that this was their favourite flower. A shamrock—they were Irish; a thistle—Scots. If there is a fireman's helmet, or a fishing boat, or a motorcycle, you have a good idea what their life's work or recreation was.

The inscription is the essence of the man or woman, a précis, if you will, of the story of their life. Some of them "died," others "passed away" or are "gone but not forgotten" or "gone to eternal rest" or "gone to be with their Saviour." Very few tell you how they died or how long they suffered. The odd one will say "lost at sea," but hundreds more, no doubt, died that way in this historic fishing community.

One stone here is shared by a husband and wife who died a week apart! It was a long time ago. There is perhaps no one alive who could tell me how they died. He died first. Did their house burn to the ground that cold winter's night? Perhaps he got her out safely but died trying to save the youngsters. Did she die of a broken heart a week later? Did she suffer unbearable pain from burns in the last week of her life?

The inevitability of death strikes me as well. One plot has identical stones, bought, no doubt, at the same time, but their final inscribed dates are thirty years apart. It's just a matter of time for all of us. Some of us do not want to think about it, yet death will come. This couple knew it and wanted to be prepared.

In another site the plot is framed by a low cement wall. On one side is a stone etched with his dates— his grave in front of it. He died in 1967—fifty-two years ago. The other side of the plot is empty—as far as I can tell—as there is no gravestone.

Was this space meant for his wife? Could she possibly still be alive? He was in his fifties when he died. Did she remarry and is buried beside another man somewhere else?

Has she been a widow for fifty years? Perhaps she is buried beside him here, but their children—if any survived—could not afford to erect a stone to her memory.

Another thing that strikes me is the continuity of life. The names I see on many of the tombstones are still in the phone book. Exactly the same names—first and last—perhaps a son, great-grandson, or cousin of the one whose grave I saw today. Hundreds of them—Bridgets, Margarets, Marys, and Annies, and Williams, Franks, Josephs, and Thomases. The Collinses, the Traverses, the Flynns, the Powers, and the Leonards.

I've now stopped at the grave of a woman who lost three young children, each about a year apart. She lived for almost sixty more years. Her grave is tidy and well-kept—no doubt by her grandchildren, the progeny of her other surviving youngsters. You don't live that long without a good reason.

I came to this graveyard today for a special reason. A friend of mine lost her young daughter in a car accident a few days ago. Her funeral is in Nova Scotia tomorrow. I am unable to attend. I wanted to come here as an act of solidarity—to peacefully ponder what my friend is facing. Tomorrow she'll be surrounded by her family, including the deceased's daughter—her granddaughter. The mother's heart is breaking.

There can be nothing in this life harder to face than the death of your child. She is strong, though. She will get past it. She has faced some very tough challenges both inside and outside the boxing ring. She has the heart of a champion. But I don't even have to tell you that she will never forget her child as long as one breath is able to pass her lips, or one beat is left in her heart. The strong, like my friend, Jennifer, will prevail.

NEWFOUNDLAND RAIN

WE ARE "BLESSED" WITH AN ABUNDANCE OF HIGH-quality rain here. Nowhere else will you find the variety, the frequency, or the inventiveness of our Newfoundland rain.

When God created rain, He wasn't sure exactly what He wanted. He needed somewhere to test the different types which He envisaged in order to choose the proper variety. Since there were no people in Newfoundland at the time—and I suspect He did not see things ever getting so bad elsewhere that any would come here—He chose Newfoundland. Somehow, it seems He never got around to eliminating the types that lost His favour.

We still regularly get horizontal rain, diagonal rain, drizzle, rain mixed with sleet, hail, snow, ice pellets, graupel (a mixture of hail and snow), fog, salt fog, and a few other things that have no meteorological name. The most common type, elsewhere, is what we here call "coming straight down out of the heavens" rain. I'm truly expecting someday to see rain coming right up out of the ground and shooting skywards.

I thought I'd seen the latter, one day last summer as I was hurrying home through the simultaneous rain and pea-soup fog. I had my camera at the ready, but when I got close enough to this peculiar display, I discovered that it was merely a lawn sprinkler! That, of course, raised another question. When is it dry enough here to set up a sprinkler without getting soaked to the skin—and why would you want to when there's no need of it?

Now, I've got nothing against rain—but how about everything in moderation? Rainbows are nice, and so is the odd thunder and lightning storm. I've seen them Upalong.

I'd just like to see one full day between the May month and the October month with sun, a slight warm breeze, but without some form of rain in your face and eyes.

I've heard tell that there are places in this province where this actually occurs. I've not, however, been lucky enough to be there on any such occasion. There's even a revered folk expression for such a day. The old people call it a "sun is splitting the rocks" kind of day. I'll believe it when I see it, so I will.

FUNERALS AND MARRIAGES

THESE ARE ABOUT THE ONLY EVENTS FOR WHICH MANY people even go to church anymore. More and more marriages these days take place outdoors or inside places other than churches. Proper thing. A hot, stuffy church wearing clothes which you wouldn't be caught alive in is not the way you want to end your life—or begin your marriage. That's one of the reasons why I've put these two ceremonies in one piece. The other reason is contrast—one of these is happy, one sad. One seems to go on forever, and the other rarely lasts very long anymore. You know which is which. I went to many of both when I was young. Being in the choir, in my father's church we had to sing at them.

At the funerals, the songs were sad and dreary and you wouldn't dare smile. The marriages were happier, the hymns more uptempo. You could smile, but you couldn't laugh if the groom bent over to pick up a dropped ring and ripped the seat out of his pants. A certain decorum was required in church.

At one funeral, the worst part was when the preacher said what a wonderful husband and father the deceased had been, when you knew the kind of reprobate he really was. Up in the choir you could look down at his beaten wife and abused children, and you knew that as bad as things had been for them, now without the few meagre dollars he ever brought home when he was through drinking, things were going to get even worse.

At marriages there is hope and a determination to work together to make life better for both participants. Sometimes it happens, other times it falls apart fast.

I got married by a Justice of the Peace—the first time. We exchanged vows on December 1 and broke up on December 23—in the same month. A short marriage, and not a happy one, but far short of a world's record.

That occurred, according to my research, in India a few years back. After saying "I do" and raising her veil to kiss the bride, he discovered she was actually his intended's grandmother! He dropped dead of a heart attack. His funeral pyre was later the same day! Two world records in one. Shortest marriage and shortest time between marriage and death. His "married bliss" was mercifully short, and the bride got to keep the dowry. Everyone won.

Turning the Last Corner on the Way Home

LIFE IS *NOT* LIKE A BOX OF CHOCOLATES. LIFE IS BEING A child arriving at the bus stop minutes after the last bus for home has gone. Due to circumstances over which you have no control, your only choice is to walk. You are on your own for the first time, with no one to guide you, and without a map. So—you start walking in the direction that seems right.

You walk down dead-end streets and have to backtrack. You come to one-way streets with no sidewalks. Most people seem to be going in the opposite direction. Everyone from whom you seek directions gives different advice. Then it starts raining, and you are unprepared. Wet and cold now, you trudge on, remembering bits and snippets of advice your parents gave you. You didn't pay enough attention at the time for these fragments to help much now.

When the weather gets worse, you want to give up but cannot. You must make it home. After what seems like forever, you see some landmarks which you recognize. You have been there before, and even if they don't lead you home, at least they provide some comfort. Soon there are fewer and fewer people from whom to seek advice. You continue on that course for a long, long time. Then, slowly, things start to look more familiar.

By now you are dead tired, but you are confident that you are heading in the right direction. Eventually there is no one at all from whom to seek advice, and you have to rely entirely on your own judgment.

You ignore the rain-turned-sleet and slog through it as it morphs into a blinding snowstorm. Finally, you come around a corner, and you recognize the back end of your neighbourhood.

Worn out and weary now, all you want is to be home. When your house appears in the distance, your spirits rise. If you can get there, even if no one is home, it will be okay. You've made it through, without any idea of how to do it—with conflicting advice and no road map.

You feel so old as you turn that last corner on your way home. You hope that your children will be as lucky—your own children who have just arrived now at the same bus stop, after their last bus for home has already gone.

PHEW! WAS THAT YOU?

I WAS LIVING IN ONTARIO IN THE LATE '60s BEFORE I SAW the light and headed back east to the home of my ancestors. Too many people in Ontario, but there were a good few from the east coast, so that made things a little more tolerable. Lil and Jack were from Pugwash, Nova Scotia.

One warm, foggy evening in the summer of 1967, Lil Connell decided to go downtown Burlington, Ontario, to the Sherwood Inn for a couple of cold draft beers. Her husband, Jack, was working the evening shift at Stelco, and her sons were out somewhere. I didn't go, as I had to study for a business test the next day.

I boarded with Jack and Lil. They were my second family. Lil was like a mother to me. So, when she called later to say her car wouldn't start and could I come down and pick her up, I was glad to help.

As we were driving home, a family of skunks—a mother and four or five young ones—strolled across the road in front of the car.

"Oh, aren't they cute, Laurie? Get me one of those!"

I knew better than to object. When Lil set her mind to something, it was going to happen. We already had two dogs and a budgie at home, but Lil was a sucker for any animal.

I pulled the car over, hopped out, and went chasing after the skunks. By now they were crossing a lawn. The mother and the first few babies sped up, but the last two dived into a bush to hide. I got one of them and took it back to Lil.

It didn't let go with its "perfume," and Lil allowed as to how it was probably too young to do so. She would take it to a vet tomorrow and get it "de-scented."

Lil held it but then put it on the floor of the car when we got home. She had to go inside to find a cage for him. I got out as well and went to help her look. We found one, and I went back to the car to capture him. He'd disappeared. And then I saw something move. He was crawling up under the dash, trying to hide behind the glove compartment.

With that, I looked up under and grabbed his back legs. I didn't see his tiny tail go up. He got me right in the face and eyes, and I flung the car door open, shouted, and ran for the house. Lil knew why, because the smell got there ahead of me.

I don't remember much about what we used to get the smell off of me. I know it involved tomato juice. My shirt was garbage, and I bathed for days to get the smell out of my hair and off my body. In about a week, I could sit at the dinner table without the kids retching. I didn't date for a longer while. The car was a different matter.

I loved my 1965 Chev Impala SS convertible. Now it stank worse than me. I left it overnight, and I guess the juices had lots of time to sink in and hunker down. The skunk had exited the open door sometime overnight, so that was a blessing. These were the days before the Internet, so I went to the drugstore to get advice.

The druggist suggested several different things, none of which worked. Slowly, the strength of the stink subsided. It was worse when you used the heater. I would leave the top down to keep the car aired out and park it in the shade so as not to fade the upholstery. I used the heater sparingly, even in winter.

When I finally sold the car, you could still smell it on a humid day. I sold it on a sunny day with the top down and one of those ever-green tree air fresheners hanging from the rear-view mirror. I know it's wrong, but I couldn't help but laugh when I thought of what might happen to the new owner.

I hope it never did, because he was a good kid, but I had to smile when I thought about it. I could picture the young guy on his first date with the girl he always wanted. They'd be parking in front of her house to say good night. She would hint that she was a little cold—just so he would put his arm around her. Being nervous and shy, he'd crank up the heater instead and out would come "eau de phew."

She'd recoil, look accusingly at him as she jumped out of his car, and as she turned to run to the house, gasp, "Phew! Was that you?"

THE MISSING HIGH SCHOOL COURSES

I LEARNED A LOT IN HIGH SCHOOL. I LEARNED THAT "A lot" is a tract of land and you can't have "a lot" of anything else. You can have much, many, a great deal of—or none, though.

But I didn't learn how to buy a "lot" or a house, or how to finance it, or anything about mortgages and interest rates. I didn't learn how to budget, how to start a business, or how to do my income taxes.

I didn't learn that if you borrow $200 from a finance company to buy an old car and pay $5 a month on the loan, you will still be paying when that car is in the junkyard, or that you might be able to finally retire the loan when you start collecting your old-age pension.

I learned about "wants and needs" and "supply and demand" in economics class but didn't learn how a consumer (a person) can control any of them. As a result, I ended up paying for "dead horses" before I figured it out—the hard way.

Our young people are borrowing $30,000, $40,000, or $60,000 for a college education. Some of these kids have never even had a bank account or ever had to work to earn their spending money. Why are we surprised when they go through their loan money like a drunken sailor and end up deeply in debt, without a degree?

At the same time, the banks are earning record profits and hold our children's lives for ransom—while writing off billions in defaulted foreign debt. The banks and/or the education system should be held accountable for the young people who fail.

What about the parents? Most of them are just learning, too. Most learned nothing about "living" when they went to high school, either. Others didn't get very far in school, and they want better for their kids. They want them to have a college education. They would give anything to make their children's lives better—easier than it was for them—so they encourage them to go into the debt of student loans.

Secondary schools are doing a reasonably good job of preparing our young people for post-secondary study. They are doing little to prepare them for life.

Don't get angry with your daughter when she drops out of college, her loan money all spent. Don't throw your son out when he has to go to work for tips and minimum wage in a fast food restaurant, with no idea how he will pay off his debt.

Get angry with the school boards, the Departments of Education, and the banks—and demand changes.

It's okay to cry along with him, though, when he tells you, "I'm sorry, Mom. It was so much money the bank put in my account. I'm so sorry. I thought it would last me forever."

YOUR COFFEE IS PAID FOR

I'VE HEARD IT REFERRED TO AS PAYING IT FORWARD, OR A random act of kindness, but there is nothing like the feeling you get the first time that someone you don't even know pays for your coffee and then drives away.

I was trying to make a right turn into a Tim Hortons in CBS, Newfoundland, one morning. Traffic lined the road in both directions. The drive-thru was so blocked that there were probably ten cars ahead of me waiting to turn in. There was one car facing us, trying to make a left into the same drive-thru lineup—a young woman in a small car.

As space became available, each vehicle ahead of me moved up quickly, not allowing her to turn in. She'd edge a little bit ahead, and every driver, man or woman, cut her off and left her stranded in her turn lane, unable to get in or escape. A high school senior on her way to school or a young woman about to be late for work at her first job?

As it got down to only two or three cars ahead of me, I thought surely someone would wave her through. Not so. How selfish are we? She was doing nothing wrong. She had as much right as those coming in the opposite direction. She's somebody's daughter. Let her through.

When I got to the head of the line, she had been there about ten minutes. The place was still blocked. I got a good look at her. She was crying. She looked about sixteen years old and perhaps had just gotten her licence.

She didn't know what to do—didn't know how to get out of this situation. I had every intention to let her in when my turn came, and I did. As I waved her through, she smiled at me through her tears.

When I got to the window to place my order, I thought about telling the lady that I would like to pay for the little blue car ahead of me. I didn't. The clerk might think I was a dirty old man hitting on this young girl. And what if the young lady refused? That would be embarrassing.

She paid for her order and drove away. She waved to me as she drove off, saluting me once again for letting her in line. When I got to the pick-up window the lady passed me my order and said with a smile, "The girl ahead of you paid for yours. She told me what you did. Thank you. She's my daughter."

THE END OF THE WORLD

SYLVIA DEE, A LYRICIST, WHO CO-WROTE WITH COMPOS-ers like Arthur Kent, wrote the lyric for "The End of the World." It was recorded in June 1962 and released in December that year by a singer named Skeeter Davis. It became a big country hit.

For years it became the theme song of broken-hearted lovers. Back in the day, if you lost your best girl/guy to another or you found out he/she was "two-timing"—cheating—on you, this was your song of solace. An instrumental version was played by Marty Stuart at Chet Atkins's funeral, and Skeeter's version was played at her own funeral in 1967.

Few of us have escaped a broken heart, or multiple cases of this condition. It is difficult, however, to tell a sixteen-year-old boy or girl, "Things will get better. You will get over it. You will have a wonderful life. I don't even remember the names of all of the girls who broke mine." You better do it, though, if you know that they're down.

Talk to your kids about suicide and about the perceived insurmountable obstacles which often later become laughable. That big tough football player has a heart as easily broken as a twelve-year-old girl's.

How many suicides over the centuries can be attributed to a broken heart? I don't know. It isn't talked about. I do know a few in my time—a couple were fine young men who could have had long and happy lives, if someone could have gotten close enough to rescue them before they drowned in despair.

It's a tragic waste of life and creates a terrible ache in the hearts of their families, an ache that just doesn't go away. An ache a million times worse than losing a cheating lover.

I understand why Sylvia Dee wrote this song and the pain she was going through. I wish, though, that it had never been recorded. This type of song had such a powerful impact on teenagers. I worry sometimes that they are inspired by the wrong lyrics written to a beautiful melody—or they misunderstand the lyric.

The only comforting thing about this particular song is that I know Sylvia had not gone through a breakup. Things aren't always what they seem, and this is a good case in point. She wrote these heartbreaking words as a loving daughter, in her late forties, inspired by the death of her dad.

— CHAPTER 7 —
ROAD WARRIORS

In the field of outside sales, the "chosen ones" who travel regularly to visit businesses are variously called sales reps, territory managers, or banner support managers. Some work part of a province or several provinces. (At one time I had everything east of Yonge Street, Toronto, with a second guy doing the rest of Canada.)

Years ago we could recognize each other by the company car—a black four-door sedan without air conditioning and often no radio. We all wore suits and ties—well, almost all, as women in this field were a rarity. In more recent years we got better cars, dressed more casually, and often your competitor was a smart, articulate woman who could open doors which you couldn't kick down.

Most years I'd put 125,000–150,000 kilometres on the car. Long days and working until late at night finishing up the paperwork. Up at 5:00 or 6:00 a.m. and gone again in the morning. We called ourselves road warriors. These are some of the stories from that five or six million kilometres as a road warrior.

HAUNTED TRUCK?

EVER SINCE I OWNED A HALF-TON AND A ONE-TON TRUCK
at my store, Grandpa Pike's, in the early 1980s, I've wanted another truck. We were now living at Carleton, in Yarmouth County,
and with a barn, outbuildings, and over 100 acres of field and forest, it
would come in handy for hauling supplies. At the time, however, I had
a four-door sedan.

My territory as area manager for Ace Hardware was Nova Scotia.
I had applied for the position while still living in Newfoundland, and
if I got the job, I hoped I could convince my new boss to let me move
to Yarmouth—instead of some more central place.

Without mentioning Yarmouth area—where I grew up—I asked
my boss did he have a specific community where he wanted me to set
up my office.

"No," he told me, "as long as you are prepared to cover the whole
province and travel five days a week, I don't care if it's Sydney or Yarmouth or somewhere in between." That's all I needed to hear!

The company was providing a car allowance at the time, and area
managers could drive any kind of car, as long as it was "a four-door
sedan in a conservative colour." I wanted a truck but said nothing
when the HR department reviewed the job description and details on
benefits—expenses, car allowance, etc.

Then one week, the vice-president (my boss), Pat Bennett, travelled with me to visit some stores in Cape Breton. Pat was in the front seat with me, and a guy from another territory, Sheldon, was in the back seat.

We started talking about the farm I'd bought, and I told Pat I wished I could afford a truck—along with the car—as it would come in handy. "Trade in your car, sure, and get a truck," he said, "as long as it's presentable."

Then from the back seat, Sheldon had his say. "But, Pat, the handbook says it has to be a four-door sedan."

I turned my head and cut him off in a loud whisper, a grin counterbalancing my words. "Shut up, Sheldon!"

The boss started laughing. The next week, I bought a truck.

The first lot I checked had a variety of makes and models in stock. I wanted something fairly new—but with the first year's depreciation gone. One truck caught my eye. It was only one model year old, had very low mileage, and had a factory cap as well.

I test drove it and went in to negotiate price. It was already underpriced, in my opinion, but I went even lower with an offer. When the sales manager accepted it, I told him I thought it was a bargain price.

"What's wrong with her?" I asked him.

"I was going to tell you before we signed anything," he said. "The reason it is priced so low is that somebody died in it. Other than that, there is nothing wrong with the vehicle."

Apparently the previous owner had hooked a hose to the exhaust, put it through the cap window, then got in the back and died. Nobody knew why he did it, but people in the whole area knew about the incident and nobody would buy the truck. The salesman said that they were about to take it out of the area and sell it at an auction, just to get rid of it.

This news did not bother me. For some reason suicide doesn't seem the same to me, as if someone had died painfully in an accident or was murdered in the truck. The man died peacefully. It was his choice. His life wasn't taken from him; he chose to end it. He died to seek relief from whatever was haunting him.

I didn't tell my wife and daughter about the truck's past until much later—after I'd sold it! I thought one of them might be spooked by its history. I drove the truck 100,000 miles or more, and even in those quiet nights I saw no ghosts nor heard any strange sounds.

Sometimes in the dark of night I'd talk to the late owner. I'd tell him I was sorry for his pain and I hoped he was at peace now. I was clipping along pretty good one night, and in the quiet darkness I heard a siren, then I saw the flashing light from the unmarked police car. I pulled over, and as he was looking at my driver's licence and registration, I joked with him, "Your ghost car has caught my haunted truck."

He asked what I meant, and after I told him the truck's story, he just handed my papers back to me. "Keep her down," he said. "One death to a vehicle is more than enough." I remembered that.

CALL HOME

I WAS SOMEWHERE EAST OF BELLEVILLE ON MY WAY TO Montreal via the 401 when I found myself following a young man driving a big sedan. My territory was southeastern Ontario, and I was the zone manager with Crest Hardware Stores. He was driving cautiously, well under the speed limit, and as I had plenty of time that day, I stayed behind him.

Suddenly there was a sharp report, like rifle fire. I thought someone was shooting at us. At the same time, I saw a burst of gravel fly away from his back passenger wheel. His tire had blown. Inexperienced and nervous, no doubt, he tried to pull off the road, not knowing what had happened. There was only a narrow shoulder—gravel then grassed down a steep bank. He lost control of the vehicle. I'm sure it flipped. This was in the 1970s, and it all happened very quickly. I wouldn't have been able to swear to it, even then. It didn't seem to roll—simply flipped. The car landed on its "feet."

There was no damage to the roof, but the fenders on one side were beat up a bit. (We found out later that the front end had some damage as well.) I pulled over and ran down into the ditch to check on him. He was fine but shaken up, of course.

"My parents are going to kill me," he kept repeating. "My parents are going to kill me."

I think they loaned him the money for the car, or he was on their insurance. He was convinced that he was a dead man when he got home. He was only about seventeen or eighteen and a high school student—a clean-cut young man. I suppose it was his first car. No doubt they had tried to drill the message of safety and caution into him, like all parents do.

I drove him down to a nearby garage, and we hired a tow truck. We went back, and once the car was towed to the garage, I told him he should call his parents.

"I can't call them. They'll kill me."

"Don't be so foolish," I told him. "They'll only be happy that you are alive and well."

He was pretty adamant that he couldn't call them. I asked what he was going to do. He didn't know. I couldn't just leave him on the side of the road. Finally, I convinced him to call. I would take him to the next service station, and we'd phone his house. If it was unsafe to go home, we'd figure out something else. He insisted I talk to them first.

His mother answered the phone.

"Your son was in accident," I told her, and before I could say anything more, she spoke.

"God, no! Is he okay? Where is he now? Is he okay?"

"He's fine," I told her. "I'll put him on in a minute. He's a little shook up, and he's a little worried. First of all, I want you to know it wasn't his fault. A tire blew. He held the car straight and tried to get off the road. I was right behind him. Unfortunately, there was no real shoulder but a deep ditch. The car's beaten up some, but he's fine. There was nothing he could do."

"His father's away, and I have no car. You sure he's okay? Can I talk to him?"

"Sure—he's right here—I'll drive him home," I told her. "I'm on my way to Montreal."

With that, I passed him the phone and walked away a bit to give him some privacy. When he got off the phone, he told me, "You were right. She didn't care about the car, but now she's worried about me."

I drove him home. He lived a couple of towns away, toward Montreal. When I got to his street, he wanted me to stop around the corner. I suspect he was concerned that his mother would react like any mother would—which would embarrass him. I gave him my card and told him that if things got rough to call my office. We didn't have cellphones yet, but I called in at work a couple times every day. I'd be able to get in touch with him.

I believe that was a Monday or a Tuesday, and when I got back to the office on Friday, I had a letter from his parents. (Canada Post was very quick in those days.) It was one of the nicest letters I have ever received. I did only what anyone would do in the circumstances, but they couldn't thank me enough. I kept that letter for years. I still have it somewhere, no doubt, and I would quote from it if I could find it.

The reason I'm writing this, though, is to say to any young person who might be reading, never be afraid to call home. Whether you've had a falling-out with your parents or not, no matter what the trouble is, never be afraid to call. Even if you've done something wrong and are in trouble with the law, call home.

Your parents' first concern is, and will always be, you—forever amen. Ninety-nine per cent of parents will walk through a brick wall for you—would take your place in death, if they could. Call home.

DOCTOR DINGWELL

I MET DAVE AT A HARDWARE SHOW/CONVENTION IN TO-
ronto the week I started work for Dominion Hardware. Dave had
been east for a few months beginning the task of developing business
for the company in Atlantic Canada. I was to join him after the show
in that function.

I was introduced to him on the show floor, but he was with a
customer, and amid all the activity and noise we had only time to
shake hands and pass pleasantries. That night, at the banquet, I was
seated at a table with seven others—all dealers who were attending
the show. A young man and his wife were on my right side, and we
introduced ourselves.

They owned a store in central Ontario. I told them I was going to
Nova Scotia to open up a new territory for the company.

"Oh, so you're going to be working with Dave Dingwell?" he asked.

"Yes," said I, "you know him?"

"He was our sales representative," the man replied.

I explained that I hadn't really had a chance to talk with him yet,
and I asked, "What's he like?"

(Doctor Dingwell is going to *kill* me for this, but here's what he
told me.)

"Well now, Dave's the kind of guy who will promise you the moon and he *might* deliver a few small meteorites!" He went on to explain that he liked him, worked well with him, but that Dave had the habit of making promises that sometimes went unfulfilled.

I was a little worried by this information, but it certainly better prepared me for the new job. After I got to know him, I came to under-stand his style, and we became close friends. It's not that Dave made promises which he did not intend to keep. Sometimes he was unable to deliver, and other times he simply forgot. Everybody knew this.

When you *really* needed something, though, Dave always came through. We worked well together, and when one of us had a good day signing up new dealers and the adrenalin was flowing, we would call the other and talk late into the night.

I was single at the time, and for several years I spent dozens of weekends at his farm in PEI. We barbecued, went fishing, took his antique farm tractor down to their sandy beach, went for drives, and in the evenings had a few cold ones.

I watched his kids grow up before I got married and had a child of my own. Along with his boys, we watched countless episodes of *The Dukes of Hazzard,* and late at night Dave and I watched many boxing matches. On Saturday nights, along with his wife and their friends, we would go to the hall in nearby Fortune for a country dance.

Our hardware dealers loved him—and especially their kids. Dave played guitar and would make up little songs with their names in them. Kids would try to crawl up on his lap. He was "Uncle Dave" to a good many of them. Still is.

We changed the territories around a couple times, and one day I found myself calling on a dealer, whose first name was Guy, in a Cape Breton store. I hadn't called on him in years, as another rep had been doing the territory. Guy was angry!

Behind his door was a pile of seven or eight McCulloch chain-saws, all defective. They had been there for months. Dave had promised to write up an authorization to return for credit, but with each visit other things came up, and he never got around to it.

A few weeks later, Dave and I were travelling together in Cape Breton and had done several presentations with prospective dealers. We got through early one day, so Dave suggested we pop in and see Guy. His store was nearby. I warned Dave that Guy was very upset and had suggested he was going to have it out with him next time he visited.

"Ah, he'll be fine," he said. When we got to the store, Dave took his guitar out of the trunk of the car. I held the store door open, and Dave went in playing and singing a radio commercial:

"You're in luck when you've got a McCulloch chainsaw,
You've got power by the hour in your hand.
With McCulloch you're the master,
Cause you keep a-cuttin' faster,
You're in luck when you've got a McCulloch chainsaw."

Guy saw and heard us come through the door. He had a shocked look on his face for a few seconds and then burst out laughing. He shook our hands and invited us to sit down. After we talked and laughed for a few minutes, he asked Dave about doing up the chainsaws on a return form.

"I'll do that in a few minutes," Dave replied. "So, what's new?"

"I have a new pool table!" said Guy, and then he invited us over to his nearby house—for a game and a drink.

We would not normally do this, but it was late afternoon and we had no more calls to make. We played guitar, played pool, drank beer and rum, and ate the takeout food that Guy ordered in. Then we started back at playing the guitar, playing pool, and drinking rum. Late into the night we found empty beds, crawled in, and slept until dawn.

In the morning, we got up quietly so as not to disturb Guy, went to our nearby car, and drove away—totally forgetting the seven or eight defective chainsaws that were still behind Guy's office door.

I gave Dave his nickname, "Doctor." Often we would team up for presentations. We would try to do these in the prospects' homes, if we could. It's usually more relaxing for clients to talk sitting around their kitchen table than crammed into a tiny office at their store—or in a hotel room.

I would appeal to the prospect's logic and business sense. Dave would talk with their kids, if any were present, or discuss non-business things that would interest the adults. If there were kids, however, and he had the guitar in the car, soon the kids were crowded around Dave, who was playing little nonsense songs and inserting their names.

Once the kids were in bed, we'd start the presentation in earnest. I'd try to get to their "head." Dave had already gotten to their "heart." Together it worked, and I began calling him the heart doctor. Finally, he became simply Doctor Dingwell.

Dave helped me out in a couple of personal crises. If he didn't save my life, he at least helped save my sanity. It is said that we are attracted to others not for their strengths but for their weaknesses. Sometimes, I believe, it is for both reasons. Their weaknesses remind us that we have our own. Their strengths, however, are what keep you together, as friends. It's been almost forty-five years now, and Dave, to me, will always be Doctor Dingwell—my brother.

Grandpa Pike with Doctor Dingwell

A Hardware Man is Good to Find

IN THE MID-SEVENTIES, I WAS TRAVELLING FOR A NATION-al hardware distributor, Dominion Hardware. We were the last of the big three to get into the Atlantic Canada market. Home Hardware had been here since the early 1960s, and Pro Hardware had a few years' jump on us, too. That didn't stop us. Some of the strongest dealers were still independent, and I worked on them to convert them to our program. It also didn't stop us from "stealing" a few dealers from the other groups, either.

I heard about Clarence Hardware from another dealer and stopped in to see them. They had only a small square footage in Saulnierville, district of Clare, on Nova Scotia's French Shore. I was living in nearby Yarmouth at the time. The manager was a short, stout, smiling guy named Gus, whom I became friends with very quickly. He was fairly new to hardware, and when I talked to him about our program, he asked a lot of questions.

Being on the seacoast, they had a market for galvanized fasteners and hardware. Galvanized hinges, nails, and bolts stand up much better to the salt air, salt fog, and in places salt spray that often envelop anything you build there. We had a great selection. Although I was a "suit," I understood hardware very well, and I think Gus appreciated the product knowledge I could give them.

On my third trip to visit him, having Gus onside, I wanted to set up an appointment with the owners to do a full presentation on the Dominion Hardware program. When I suggested it to him, his smile faded. He told me that I was too late.

The owners had signed with Pro Hardware. I wanted to know if it was definitely too late. He told me that the new store fixtures and the opening stock order had already been done—and the papers signed.

I suppose I looked disappointed, because I surely was. Often it takes six or eight calls to get to a presentation, especially with an absentee owner. You need to have the manager onside first, or he can kill your chances. The Pro guy hadn't considered that and had gone directly to the owners. Gus was brought in only when the deal was already done.

Then Gus surprised me. He wanted to call the owner, who was at his fish plant nearby, and at least have him meet me. Clarence, the owner, came over at once. Clarence was a big man, always smiling as well, and we immediately took to each other. His two daughters were partners, and he thought that although a deal had been made elsewhere, at least they should meet me. I agreed to go to his house that night and meet with the three of them.

I arrived at 7:00 p.m. The first question he asked me was what I thought of Gus—was he knowledgeable enough and skilled enough to operate a franchised store? I praised Gus because I liked him, liked the way he interacted with the customers, and how he would listen to advice. I told Clarence I would assist with the set-up, work closely with Gus, and help to make him a better manager, if I had the opportunity.

Clarence liked the idea that I lived nearby and appreciated the kind of flexibility that our program provided. Gus had already mentioned my company to him and had told him our pricing was good, our selection right for their market, and delivery was fast. The daughters asked questions as well, and both seemed to like what they were hearing, too.

We talked for hours as we got to know each other, and I genuinely liked the man. I regretted that I was unable to speak in French, but they were fluently bilingual. I had only high school French and no practice. About 11:00 p.m., Clarence suddenly jumped up and said, "*Ça Suffit!*"

I knew what that meant. Literally, "that is sufficient." He'd heard enough. It was time to leave. As I started gathering up my materials, I learned that it was his way of saying, "That's enough, you've convinced me!"

To make a long story short, the next morning he called Pro Hardware and told them to cancel the opening order—and his contract—and they agreed. I called the fixture company, as the fixtures—invoiced through Pro—had already been shipped. They changed the invoicing to Dominion Hardware, and I had a new store!

Gus was happy when he got the news the next morning, and I owed that new store to him. Had he not called Clarence, just so I could meet him, it would never have happened. I worked with Gus that day to do a new opening order. Gus and I looked at our 30,000 items on an old microfiche reader until well into the evening, but we got it done. I'd punch in the number on the MSI ordering device, and he would say, "Pass me six of those."

I always kidded Gus about how he would use the word "pass" for "send" whenever he ordered product, but I "passed" him millions of dollars worth of hardware over the years and truly enjoyed calling on him. If the Pro guy had gotten to Gus's heart instead of just his boss's, I would have had no chance.

He knows a lot more about hardware now than I do. I'll never forget what he said to me when I told him that Clarence and the girls had decided to go with me. As he shook my hand, he said, "A hardware man is good to find."

LOBSTER!

I LOOK AFTER MY CARS NOW, BUT YEARS AGO WHEN THEY gave me a new company car every year or two—not so much. When you are driving 125,000–150,000 kilometres per year and working sixteen-hour days, you sometimes neglect to do regular maintenance. Practically living in my car, there'd be empty coffee cups, discarded fast food containers, empty cigarette packs, and cigarette butts that fell out of an overflowing ashtray, covering much of the floor.

Most times I cleaned it out on the weekends. If I got home early enough on Friday, I'd get an oil change and have the fluid levels checked. The new car warranty was gone within months of getting the vehicle, and the big boss, "Moose," was always nagging us to keep down expenses. When you have an outside sales job and your territory comprises a couple provinces, that is not so easy to do. The only way to avoid a tank of gas a day, three meals, and a hotel room would be to stay home. I tried to save expenses on maintenance.

The big boss, Moose didn't consider the millions in sales you were adding to the territory, but only about whether he could get $5,000 or $6,000 for the car when he traded it in. When he'd see a salesman's car pull into the parking lot, he would be down in a flash, checking the air pressure in the tires, looking for dents and scratches, etc.

He'd bellow like a bull moose in rutting season (that's why we called him moose). "The car! The car! What have you done to the car?" That stuff gets tiresome when you've driven 1,800 kilometres to get to a sales meeting and your sales are up fifty per cent or more from the previous year. I decided that at the next sales meeting I'd have some fun with him.

That spring, it was muddy on the back road where I lived, and then came a hot, dry spell and the mud baked on. The day before I left for the meeting in Toronto, I was in downtown Halifax on business. I parked the car in the area where Historic Properties is now, near the waterfront. I left the windows down.

When I got back, I noticed that seagulls had defecated on the roof and hood, and a couple of them were still in the car, rooting through my garbage. I regained possession of the car and drove home to key in a couple large sales orders and transmit them to our head office computer by phone.

I know I should have stopped to clean the car, but the next morning I had to leave early for Toronto, so I went home, did my paperwork, and went to bed. As I was just across the New Brunswick border the next morning, I spotted a sign advertising LIVE AND BOILED LOBSTER.

Ontario people love lobster. They would kill or die for lobster, and they think we eat it every second meal. If you want to suck up to the boss, neither increased sales nor lower expenses will work as well as a half-dozen two-pound bottom-feeding scavengers.

I took the beer out of my cooler, filled it with the boiled lobster, and packed it tight with ice. I figured I'd replace the ice in northern New Brunswick, and again in the morning, when I checked out of the hotel at Quebec City. I totally forgot the lobsters until my nose reminded me the next day, when I stopped at a traffic light in Montreal. I knew it was too late to save the lobster, and I decided to dump them as soon as I got through the city.

When I got back to highway speed on the M-C Freeway west of Montreal, the smell receded. I didn't think of the lobsters again until

I stopped for gas near the Ontario border. I went around and opened the trunk. If you have not smelled lobster rotting on a hot day, think about what the stuff they eat smells like.

Does anyone know how houseflies can get into the closed trunk of a car travelling at sixty miles an hour—and make babies? You get the picture. I slammed the trunk shut and decided to dump the whole thing, cooler and all, at the very next rest stop. I didn't dare do it here. There were just too many adults around—and poor innocent children.

There was a big oil barrel garbage can at the next rest stop and hardly anyone around, so I dumped the whole mess quickly and sped away. Did I forget to tell you the cooler had tipped over and water was sloshing around in the trunk? I figured it would be dried up and the smell dissipated by the time I got to Toronto. I was wrong, of course.

I slept in the car that night—or tried to—and the smell went through me and everything in my suitcase. I pulled into the office parking lot at 7:45 a.m., in good time for the sales meeting at eight. I saw Moose looking out the window, and he was outside nearing my car before I could escape.

"The car," he bellowed, his voice a touch higher and thinner than normal. "Oh my God, what's happened to the car?"

"Oh, that's nothing," I responded, thinking he was referring to the white splotches, "that's just seagull shit." Then I realized he was referring to the smell to which I was now getting accustomed. He shivered and shook, his face went pale, then red again, and I knew I was skating on thin ice.

"Oh, you mean the smell?" I said offhandedly. "I brought you up a feed of lobster, boss, but they went bad in the trunk."

A look resembling pity and then regret came over his face as his whole body relaxed.

"That's a shame, but thanks anyway," he offered lamely and walked back into the building, a defeated man.

THE MOTEL

I'D BEEN DRIVING ALL DAY THROUGH A SNOWSTORM. Why? Because I'm stupid. The blizzard was getting worse as the wind came up and darkness fell. Out in rural New Brunswick, there weren't a lot of places to stop. I knew there was a good motel if I could make it to the next town. The driving got worse on the unplowed secondary road. There were no other cars. I still had an hour to drive, and if I were to stop, I would surely bog down. Then, mercifully, I saw some streetlights, a scattered house, and then at a bend in the road (thank you, God, I'll never sin again), a motel!

I could see no sign. The parking lot was drifted in, but it was obviously a motel—two wings of rooms in a wide "V" shape. Then I saw the small lighted sign over the door in the middle that read OFFICE. I rammed the car through the snow and got almost up to the office door before she bogged down. With my briefcase and suitcase, I trudged up the steps and entered.

It looked like they had available rooms, as I had only seen two or three cars outside, drifted in with snow. In the lobby was a snack machine, a pop cooler, a couple of upholstered easy chairs, and a big oak desk, at which sat the oldest woman in the world. She looked up at me quizzically as I walked over to her.

'Some storm, eh?" I said.

"Yes," she laughed, as she studied me and my luggage, but said nothing more.

"Can I get a room for the night?" I wondered aloud.

This time she really broke out in a gale of laughter and had to steady herself on the chair. When she quit shaking and rubbing her eyes, she looked back at me and asked, "How old are you, son?"

I was cold. I was tired. I was wet, as the snow on my clothes was starting to melt. I wanted a room, not a relationship. I would have asked her what business it was of hers but quickly thought better of it. I was stuck here. There was no other motel around. She was just a lonely old woman, I figured. Next she will tell me her age.

"I'm thirty-two," I said with a forced smile.

"I'm sorry, son. You're too young," she managed to say through laughs and giggles. Finally composing herself, she told me, "This here is a senior citizens' home!"

By now a few seniors were gathering in the lobby, getting ready for supper, and the owner came out from his living quarters behind the office. It didn't take long for him to decide that he couldn't let me go back out into the storm. So, they gave me a room, fed me supper, and I joined in telling stories by the fireplace and singing around the piano, afterwards. In a community with few choices, this was the absolute best place I could have stopped.

They didn't ask for anything, but I gave them the going hotel rate for the room and my supper. In the morning, with the storm gone and the lot plowed, I headed back out on the road. I hope it's a long time before I have to live in a seniors' home, but if it is as good as it was for me the night I was stranded, it won't be all bad, I s'pose.

GETTING TRACTION

SOMETIMES A NEW STORE TAKES OFF SLOWLY. FOR VARI-
ous reasons it may take a while to "get traction." That's what happened to our new Dominion Hardware store in Riverview, New
Brunswick. They had a good inventory, a prime location, and a great
showroom, but sales were growing too slow. At the time I had left my
job at Dominion and had bought and was operating Grandpa Pike's,
my own building supply store at the other end of Albert County.

My old boss at Dominion asked me if I would consider coming back
to work part-time as a consultant. I agreed, and as my first project he
asked me to find out what was wrong with the Riverview store and fix it.
I did a lot of planning and phoning in the evenings, but I was only away

from my own store one day a week. I talked to the staff and the managers to get their ideas on what was wrong. Their ideas, many of which I used, were good. As a result, we expanded "open" hours, re-merchandised several departments, and added new product categories.

In addition to that I started "Ladies' Night," one night a week, as a way to increase the female traffic. These evenings, we had on hand an expert in a different product group to do a short seminar. We had an electrician, a plumber, a painter, a flooring guy, and others. We offered free coffee and doughnuts and specials that were good for that evening only. We attracted many women, and a good few of them became regular shoppers.

We also ran a sale each week and did other special promotions. Grandpa Pike came in a couple of Saturdays wearing his cowboy hat and did free shoeshines. A portable sign was set up outside, with the message changed daily. Finally, we got some traction.

The store was well on its way to profitability when a young couple approached me and wanted to buy our store, Grandpa Pike's, in Riverside–Albert. At the time, Dominion needed someone as territory manager in Nova Scotia and wanted me to take the job—full-time. So, we sold the business, and I went back on the road for them. I lost track of Riverview and gave up consulting, as this new job was all-consuming of my time.

I have only one small regret about leaving the Riverview project, though. I had a major promotion planned for the peak of the gardening season, and I never got to do it. I had a truckload of product ordered, a great retail price, a big banner painted, and arrangements made to borrow a cow from a local farmer. I was all ready for an attention-grabber.

The plan was to have a tractor-trailerload of bagged cow manure in the parking lot, near the busy roadway. Grandpa Pike in his cowboy hat and cane would be out front and centre. He'd parade back and forth with the cow (wearing a bell) on a leader, carefully stepping around cow-pies. Above me the big banner on the truck would read: CAN YOU BUY FRESHER? I think it would have been a traffic stopper.

DODGING THE SCALES

IN 1999, MY WIFE, KATIE, AND I DECIDED TO MOVE BACK
to Newfoundland. She gave up her real estate career, and I gave up my
position as area manager for a major paint manufacturer. We sold the
house in New Brunswick in early 2000 and, already working in Newfoundland, I went back to New Brunswick to help pack and to move our
household goods to the new home we'd bought in Conception Bay South.

I rented the biggest U-Haul truck, with a twenty-six-foot box and
an attic over the cab, but I knew all our goods would not all fit on the
truck. They didn't have a trailer I could rent. This was not my first
rodeo, though, so I knew how to pack, and pack tight. We had a big
house full of furniture, Katie had enough craft materials to open a
store, and I had an extensive collection of antique tools, hardware, and
farm equipment.

When I was through, we had the truck packed so tightly that a
stowaway mouse would have had to take short, shallow breaths. She
was truly loaded to the gunwales. The tires weren't flat, but any trucker
worth his salt could tell at a glance by how low she sat that she was way
overweight.

Driving a commercial vehicle, you have to stop at all the government weigh scales. I considered going to one of the freight carriers in
Moncton, where they have their own scales, to see how much she was

over. I decided not to, though, as I would have no defence in the event I was stopped, if I already knew she was too heavy.

I'd heard horror stories from truckers who had to unload, by hand, at a weigh scale and redistribute the load—leaving the excess cargo to be picked up by their company—not to mention the fines. My strategy was to get as far as I could by avoiding scales, and if I got caught to plead innocence and beg mercy. (I had no way of knowing in absolute certainty that she was overweight.) Many scales close down at night and in tougher economic times open and close at random hours to catch truckers off-guard and to cut costs.

We left early in the morning, in the dark, my wife driving the car—packed to the gunwales itself—and me at the wheel of the U-Haul. The first scale, at Amherst, just into Nova Scotia, had not yet opened for the day, and we just breezed by. The next one was at Enfield, just north of the airport on the 102. We skirted around it by using the old highway. The third challenge was at the Canso Causeway. I pulled in at the Tim Hortons just before the scale, and Katie scouted ahead to see if the "Vehicle Compliance Centre" was open. She circled back and gave me the thumbs-up, and we rolled on into Cape Breton.

We got the evening crossing by ferry from North Sydney to Port aux Basques and arrived on Newfoundland soil about 1:00 a.m. About ten minutes up the road was the next scale. Just as the god of all truckers, professional and amateur, would decree, this one was closed for the night.

We only had three more scales to run. Pynn's Brook near Corner Brook was easy, as it was closed, too. At Grand Falls it was a different story. Open. This one was lined up with trucks in both directions.

In the yard were several rigs being unloaded and several inspectors' vehicles with their lights flashing. It looked like it was going to be a long time, and these tired, overworked guys would throw the book at us when we drove onto the scale.

There was nothing we could do but wait. As the lineup grew longer, annoyed truckers honked horns, some walking up to the scale and complaining—especially those headed to the boat. Finally, an employee from the scale came down onto the highway and started waving any truckers who were running empty out of the lineup and on through. I believe he may have been waving the big Day and Ross truck behind me to bypass the scale, not me, but I put my signal on, avoided eye contact, and pulled past him and on through.

Looking back in my mirror, I could see him waving out a Midland truck and another empty one, so I kept on "trucking." I guess he just assumed that I misunderstood and let it go. I'm not a professional trucker, so what do I know? One more scale to go!

Goobies, just east of Clarenville, was the last scale. Once past that, it was only about an hour and a half to the first exit for CBS. Almost 1,200 kilometres so far, and six scales, and we had yet to be "weighed in the balance and found wanting." We stopped at Clarenville to eat, rest, and gas up, as I knew that if the scale was open at Goobies, we might be a long time getting away.

It was open. There were a few trucks coming and going. It looked like just a normal day. I rolled up onto the scale and then moved ahead for the back axle, and as I came off the scale the flashing red light came on. I was waved over to the side, and a uniformed guy with a clipboard came up and asked me to get out of the cab. I got out.

It was starting a light drizzle, and rain was forecast. I was thinking, how big is the fine, and what will I do with the stuff I have to take off?

"What in the hell are you hauling on that thing?" he began.

"Are we overweight?" I asked him.

"Overweight? You've got enough on there for a tractor-trailer!"

I was tired and worn out from driving. I'm sure I looked worried, and then he asked, "What are you hauling?"

"My whole life, sir. Everything," I said as politely as I could. "My wife's behind me there in that car, drove crazy with the dog and cat and a car full of household goods, and I've got all our furniture, dishes, clothing, tools, food, and everything else we've collected in a lifetime on the mainland, chasing jobs and bad promises. Everything I own in this world is on that truck. We're moving back."

"Where are you coming from?" he asked, his voice softening a little, his scowl less threatening.

"Moncton, sir."

"Moncton? You've come all the way from Moncton and they didn't stop you at the scales anywhere?"

"No, sir," I said, "they just waved us through."

"How far are you going?"

"As far as CBS," I told him.

"And you're coming back home to live?"

"Yes, sir."

"Then go on, b'y," he said with a grin as he walked on back toward the office.

I saw him smile and nod at Katie as he went by and the look of relief sweep over her face. As I pulled out on the highway, I lit up my pipe and started singing an old trucker's song by Dave Dudley, "Six Days on the Road." *I'm gonna make it home tonight.*

KICKING YOU WHEN YOU ARE DOWN

JUST A MILE OR SO WEST OF CLARENVILLE, NEWFOUND-land, on the TCH is a long uphill stretch that at the time was deeply rutted from heavy trucks. You had to be careful if it was raining due to the danger of hydroplaning. The cop told me later that three or four vehicles had gone off the road there in the last couple months.

Leaving from St. John's at 5:00 a.m., I'd just taken the exit into Claren-ville to pick up a Timmies. It was now just before seven when I pulled back out on the highway. I ended up in the ditch. She landed on her "feet," and the only damage was a flat tire and a bent fender. I hitchhiked back into Clarenville and found a tow truck. When we got back to remove my car, a policeman was just getting back in his cruiser, presumably after checking my vehicle to make sure there was no one injured inside.

As the tow guy and I got into the ditch, I was shocked to see that the driver's-side rear window had been smashed out. I was absolutely certain it was intact when I left the scene. I had also power-locked the doors upon leaving. Then it hit me. My briefcase, which I always kept on the floor behind the driver's seat, was gone. There was a big rock on the back seat and shards of broken glass everywhere.

While buddy towed the car into his garage, I talked with the cop, who filled out a police report. There was no money in the briefcase, but it contained my agenda book.

In that little binder I also kept my chequebook, a few credit cards which I did not use regularly, a couple of lottery tickets, and the contact information of everyone in my business and private life.

My licence, my regular credit cards, and cash I kept in my wallet. Then I thought, *Where is my wallet?*

I remembered putting it up on the dash after the stop at Tim Hortons. It was gone! Would the thief break into the back seat, then somehow reach up front to the dash to take my wallet? He must have, as all the other doors were still locked. I unlocked the front door and sat in the driver's seat, trying to see if I may have moved the wallet later and forgotten. I found it! It had come off the dash and fallen in the pocket on the door.

With his report written, and not much confidence from the officer about the likelihood of recovering my briefcase, I accepted a ride with him to the garage. The garage replaced the blown tire with my spare, bent out the fender so it wasn't scraping, and, after checking everything for safety, gave me the car back. While they were doing this work, I contacted 1-800 numbers to freeze my bank account and cancel the credit cards that had been in my agenda book. I had to contact the insurance people, go back to St. John's and get another car, and deal with all the inconvenience and aggravation that goes with an unplanned event like this.

I always buy the same numbers in Lotto 6/49. On the way home, reasoning that if the missing tickets won anything the thief would cash them in, I replaced them. I figured that if they did win anything with them, then I would also win and go to the police. It would be wonderful if a thief got caught by this one chance in many millions. Unfortunately, my bad luck held, and when the draws came I won nothing.

I'm telling you all of this, but I have only one question. Maybe you know the answer.

What kind of a human being would walk up to a car in the ditch and, after checking to make sure no one saw them, decide that this poor son of a bitch needed more grief today, and rob anything of value remaining?

DOES ANYONE SMOKE?

THERE WERE ONLY A FEW TIMES I HAD TO DEAL WITH really bad news during my career in outside sales. This was one of the worst of them.

It was a sad day for me when it was announced that hardware distributor Sodisco-Howden was buying out my employer, Ace Canada. All our outside staff had been called to head office in Markham, Ontario, for an announcement. Rumours had been flying for weeks that the two companies were in final talks.

Consolidation in the hardware industry was ongoing, and these two distributors had gone toe to toe fighting for the independent dealers' business. Neither Ace nor Sodisco-Howden had enough business to hold on alone. When Home Hardware bought Molson's Beaver Lumber chain—Ace's chief customer—the speculation and rumour heightened.

In fact, I had been drawn to Ace Canada by a different narrative about a year earlier. At that time I was working in Newfoundland with my own agency, Blackwood Marketing. The rumour was very strong that Ace was buying Sodisco-Howden, not the other way around. This made sense, and when Ace's sales territory in Nova Scotia became vacant, I applied and got the job. I mothballed Blackwood Marketing, sold our house, and moved my family to Nova Scotia. Now a scant thirteen months later, another move was imminent.

Since the ongoing rumours had always been that Ace was doing the buyout, I didn't want to believe any differently. I drove up from Nova Scotia.

When I arrived at head office, the sombre mood of everyone reflected my own. At the last minute the announcement was delayed for a few hours, and as we waited and waited, the atmosphere didn't get any better.

When the announcement finally came, early evening in the cafeteria, several employees immediately burst into tears. Many, like me, had only been with the company a short time, and in addition their income was critical for their families—mortgages, young children. Others of us, although expecting it, were stunned and stood silently while listening to the usual platitudes of "business as usual," "no job losses," etc.

We all knew in our hearts that our office and distribution centre would close and that outside jobs in sales and banner support, like mine, would simply be absorbed by their outside sales guys. There had to be "efficiencies gained," or a buyout made no sense.

Sure enough, those changes occurred in rapid succession, and all of those dreaded things happened. I didn't wait for them to "come and get me." I started looking for another position right away. Some guys did wait for the other shoe to fall and wound up out of work. I decided to go back to Newfoundland and reactivate Blackwood Marketing with a couple of lines, and within a month I gave my notice and moved back there.

That's just business, you might say. That's true, of course, but it wasn't just the news. It was also the coldness exhibited by the new owner in the next two days after the announcement.

Ace's outside sales guys were asked to wait around and be interviewed by an executive of Sodisco-Howden. He would hold a group meeting tomorrow, and then interview each one of us separately the rest of that day and on the following day. We all worked for the rest of the day creating or polishing up our resumés.

The next morning, buddy didn't show up, so we waited again. And I mean just waited—there was nothing else to do. (We had no offices, as we were field people who worked out of our homes.) We sat in any empty chair we could find to try to pass the time. He showed up around noon, unshaven and dishevelled, looking like the Trivago guy who'd been living in his car for a month. He called us all together for the general meeting.

He started off with, "I don't know how many jobs there are going to be. I don't know how many changes we will make. Some of you guys may not even want to work for us, and if you don't, that's fine. You can leave now if you want to." I was stunned with the cold, uncaring attitude. Then he continued on with a few more words.

He was going to meet with each of us individually, but he didn't know in what order. (So, we couldn't go back to the hotel and wait our turn.) Then he asked, "Does anybody smoke?"

A few of the guys did, but not knowing whether that was a fireable offence to him, no one raised their hand—except me.

"Good," says buddy, "I need a smoke, so I'll start with you. Let's go outside."

We went out through a breezeway to a door that led to the employee parking lot, with office staff coming and going.

Standing there on the steps in the wind was where I had my interview. He didn't want to see the resumé I'd worked on the afternoon and evening before. He said nothing that he hadn't said to the group.

The interview lasted as long as it took him to smoke half a cigarette. I got my pipe filled but didn't have time to smoke it. He went back in. I went out to my car, smoked my pipe, and tried to make sense of his attitude.

I almost drove away and back to Nova Scotia. Then I remembered

I'd left my briefcase inside, so I went back in. I ran into my old boss with Ace, Pat Bennett. Pat is about as nice a man as you might be fortunate enough to meet. He calmed me down. I stayed, with nothing to do, until we were dismissed to go home the following day.

The president of Sodisco-Howden conference-called us later and apologized for the treatment, but he didn't fire the guy. I suspect that he was simply doing damage control.

I suppose they didn't want us to walk out until they knew all our customers and picked our brains. Business is tough. I agree with that, but there is no need of dumping humiliation on distressed and discouraged people who know that they will soon lose their jobs. What's it cost to show a little kindness, common courtesy, or some empathy?

Less than a year later, though, I got a call from the regional manager at Sodisco-Howden, and without an interview but with the salary and conditions that I insisted on, I was hired to take over their Newfoundland territory. Without dips in the road, there would be no high spots. I met a few "dips" along the way, no mistake.

I'll Fly Away / Sister Beulah

LET ME TELL YOU HOW I LEARNED THAT SONG.

It was the summer of 1965. My best friend, Peter, and I hitchhiked from Toronto to Mexico City. Travelling through the Deep South, we were stranded of a Sunday evening on a quiet two-lane blacktop. We walked until we came to a crossroad. Our map indicated that if we went down that red dirt road about ten miles we would come to the four-lane. We commenced to walk, and we passed shacks and shanties in that black community and saw the worst kind of poverty—the kind where folks had all but given up.

After a mile or so, we heard the sound of a vehicle approaching. We turned to see a big red rooster tail of dust coming up behind us as that 1950s-vintage, beat-up pickup slowly drew abreast.

The old black gentleman pulled over and glanced in quick succession at our city clothes, our backpacks, our outstretched thumbs, and finally at our pale white faces. He was wearing a black tie on a white shirt, and there was a Bible on the bench seat beside him. "You boys lost?" he asked us. "No, sir," I said, glancing at his Bible, "I believe *I'm* saved—but my friend here is a pretty bad sinner!"

His face broke into a toothy grin, and he laughed slow and easy, like we were old friends. "Git in! Git in!" he told us. "Y'all came to the right place!"

"I'll drive you through to the highway after church. They's a big truck stop out there. Here's our church, just ahead. We be coloured, but you boys is welcome."

The sanctuary was packed. Peter and I were the only whites. The service was about to begin. Our new friend was a deacon/usher, and he seated us before going to the back. A gracious middle-aged lady beamed a welcoming smile and passed us a hymn book.

"I'm Sister Beulah," she said as she slid over to make room. I can't remember much about the inside of the church or the preacher, and I don't remember the name of the deacon, but I'll *never* forget Beulah!

She couldn't have been more accommodating had she been welcoming royalty. Her big round face shone, and her eyes sparkled. She sat alone, but a narrow gold band on her ring finger indicated she was married.

I wondered if she had a boy or two, our age, fighting in Vietnam, or maybe her kids had gone to work up north in the big factories of Detroit or Chicago. They weren't sending much home, though, as her clothes were worn and threadbare.

She was wearing her best brooch on the yellowing collar of a white blouse, and a big-brimmed straw hat sat at a jaunty angle on her salt-and-pepper curls. It was quite evident that the church was the highlight of her very life.

Toward the end of the service they started singing, "I'll Fly Away."

She was singing her heart out and clapping along with the music, and I glanced over as tears streamed down her cheeks. The look of joy and peace on that lady's face was simply *unforgettable*. Let there be no doubt, that sister knew just *exactly* where she was going someday.

I'd seen enough on our trip through the south to tell that it contrasted pretty well with where she'd been. When they got to the chorus where everyone else was singing "O Glory," she was singing "Sweet Jesus," and the tears were still rolling down her wonderful face.

I never saw Sister Beulah again after that evening. When church was over, we lined up with a number of others for a drink of cool well water from an enamel dipper by the outside well. The deacon gave us our ride out to the highway, stopped his truck, bowed his head, and prayed for our safety before we left. By the next night we were a few hundred miles closer to Mexico.

That was many, many years ago—but sometimes now when I go down a dirt road I think about Sister Beulah, long since gone to her reward, no doubt.

And whenever I hear that song, I'm reminded of Beulah and the countless millions of faithful, like her, who had so *precious little* on this earth but still praised God.

And whenever I sing it, I sing, "Sweet Jesus."

HOME HARDWARE

I WAS IMPRESSED WITH THE PEOPLE AT HOME HARDWARE right from the first time I went through the front door at the Debert, Nova Scotia, facility. Everyone spoke to me. Everyone smiled. I felt instantly "at home." I had recently been hired as Dealer Development Manager, Atlantic, with the specific mission of adding new members to the group.

In that role, I would be visiting independent dealers in markets where we needed stores, with the goal of finding worthy candidates and bringing them into this dealer-owned co-operative. I would also be meeting with individuals interested in selling their business and, after assessing the business, finding an existing Home member or outside candidate who was able to buy it and convert it to a Home store.

I'd done this kind of work for most of my career in hardware/building materials, but not as a stand-alone job. I'd always functioned as a territory manager as well, supervising existing stores. To be able to focus, full-time, on recruiting new stores to a major banner was my dream job.

After a series of meetings with different departments, I was given a tour of the distribution centre. As we walked through the door from the cafeteria to the warehouse, a shift of workers was coming in for their coffee break. I've visited many factories and DCs over the years, and in many cases the warehouse people avoid "the suits."

Here they all smiled and spoke, and everyone was on a first-name basis. I was so impressed with the quality and attitude of all the employees, warehouse and office, that it made my "selling" them to outsiders much easier to do.

From day one I knew that if I could get a prospect to visit our regional office or our head office in St. Jacob's, Ontario, they would not only be impressed with the size and scope of the operation but, after meeting our people, would be convinced they were about to make a wise decision. Several months later I attended my first market (buying show) with Home, held at St. Jacob's.

It was the best-organized, -operated, and -attended show I had seen in my forty-some years in the business. Meals were served right at the show in a huge cafeteria set up specifically for the purpose. Four lines of buffet, several choices of entrees, and a wide selection of desserts at lunchtime. The room must have held a thousand, and a sea of red coats and jackets moved endlessly in and out of the room.

The place was packed. I was alone with a full tray, looking for an empty seat. I finally spotted one and, when I got close, was waved in by the big friendly man sitting opposite. He was an older guy, and he was talking with a young woman and her boy who were sitting beside him. They were discussing farming, horses, and a charity that she was representing at the show. He had finished eating just before I arrived. Shortly after, he excused himself and went back out to the show floor.

I ate quickly so that I could get back to my booth as well, as we had some prospective members arriving. In the three years I worked with Home, we invited many prospects to the show, and I believe there was only one who chose not to join our organization. In the Atlantic, we added twenty-one stores in that time. I had some wonderful times with Home. I wish it could have gone on forever.

The moment I remember most, though, was that young lady and

her kid—just a simple country woman at the show to raise some charitable funds—and her amazement at how nice the people were. It was, I suspect, the biggest event she had ever attended. I won't forget the last few words we spoke together. When the Home guy was gone, noticing I too was wearing a red Home blazer, she turned to me and said, "Wow, what a nice man. I'm not even a dealer, and he had all the time in the world for me. He knows all about horses, and he was so nice to my son. What does he do with Home Hardware?"

"He runs it," I told her. "That's the president, Paul Strauss."

She was getting up to leave as we spoke these few words, and as she left, she shook her head, smiled again, and said, "Wow!"

That pretty well sums up my whole experience at Home Hardware: Wow!

— CHAPTER 8 —

WHEN I WAS YOUNG

These are tales of my school days and into my early twenties. The Great Depression may have ended in the bigger centres with the outbreak of World War II, but in the small rural areas of the Atlantic Provinces they persisted through the 1950s and for some into the early 1960s. I didn't have a particularly happy childhood, but I won't bore you with those stories. These are some of the happy memories.

GARTH HATFIELD'S

IN THE 1950s, WE LIVED ON A GRAVEL ROAD, OVER A HALF-hour drive from Yarmouth, Nova Scotia. I was about fourteen. During the school year, we went to town daily on the school bus. During the summer months, however, the trips were much less frequent. The kids worked in the gardens, or taking care of the chickens, or cutting firewood, or tearing up stumps, or digging out rocks. During the summer, it was all work. We'd work, sleep, and then work some more, in a seemingly endless cycle.

I can still feel that hot summer sun on my back and my brush-cut head—and still see the clouds of dust which passing cars launched toward our home place. We also picked blueberries and sold them. In the evenings we'd search for the pop and beer bottles which those passing vehicles would discard into the ditches. There were always rum and beer bottles, as we were near the end of the road—and drivers wanted to get rid of the "evidence" before getting to the more patrolled pavement. These were the activities which provided my "going to town" money. It was only pennies, but they slowly added up.

Every second or third week, we'd go to Yarmouth on Saturday evening to buy groceries and other supplies. Going to town for a few hours was what a trip to Disneyland or two weeks of summer camp was to many kids, I suppose. It was a major deal to us. We cleaned up from the day's work, ate supper early, and put on our best clothes. The excitement built as you got closer to town with all the cars and people, the sounds and smells of the city.

The old man would park downtown, and he and my mother and the younger kids would go to the Royal Store. My two older sisters would sometimes meet their friends, or window-shop for things they couldn't afford to buy in the clothing and sundries departments.

My older brother would go to a bookstore or two. I'd head right over to Garth Hatfield's, almost across from the old Royal Store. Garth and his wife operated a confectionery/magazine/tobacco store. You could smell the candy, gum, and chocolate bars before you even got close. I'd ignore that and go directly to the magazines. If I could afford to, I'd buy a boxing magazine—either *The Ring* or *Boxing Illustrated-Wrestling News*.

At home, I had a homemade heavy bag stuffed with old shoes and clothing, hanging from a tree limb just inside the woods. Any free time I'd get—which was scarce if the old man was home—I'd go there and beat the hell out of it. It was a surrogate for my father, and I intended, when I got big enough and strong enough, to lay a beating on him and then leave home. I never did it, but it was a dream that kept me going.

Garth was a big, round-faced man. He never said much. He'd smile and nod and stay close to the cash register. At Garth's I'd weigh the value of the magazines by checking the number of pages, the profiles of boxers, the photos and stories of recent fights, and decide which one to buy.

I was in there often enough that he knew me. Although he closely watched a few other people who came in, I'll always believe that Garth knew I wasn't going to steal from them. I ended up spending all my money there.

He never said a word while I read many of the articles in the one magazine which I *didn't* buy. I guess that's a form of stealing, but nothing was ever said. If I had enough left after the magazine, I'd get a box of Cracker Jack.

That syrup-coated popcorn and peanut mixture was my favourite treat. If I was really rich that week, I'd also buy a bottle of Nesbitt's Orange. Usually, though, I had only enough for a magazine. When I got my first part-time job—at the Royal Store—I went to Garth's almost daily. Later I started smoking, and reading newspapers, and I bought it all at Garth's. The heck with the price. I went elsewhere only if Garth didn't carry it.

I stopped hating my father, but all these years later, with both my old man and Garth long gone, it's Garth that I'd rather see again. If I could, I'd thank him for looking the other way when I read too much of a magazine I couldn't afford to buy. I'd thank him for looking away when I was shopping. He knew instinctively, I suppose, that I wouldn't steal from him. He was a good man. He showed me that the same measure of respect or trust that you afford an honest adult is also due a teenager.

"Can What You Can Can and Eat What You Can't"

I WOULDN'T SAY IT WAS A MANTRA, BUT IT WAS DEFINITE-
ly an unwritten rule when I was growing up. I'm speaking of fruit,
vegetables, and other food products. Some people had freezers in the
late 1950s and early '60s, but many of us didn't even have a refriger-
ator. We had a fridge most times, but not at one house where we lived
during my early teens. It had no electricity—or plumbing.

Rural folks dried, smoked, salted, or canned everything they could
get their hands on. My mother canned 200 to 300 quart jars every
summer and fall—everything from plums, pears, apples, jams, jellies,
and berries, to pickles, pickled beets, fresh beets, turnip greens, beet
greens, beans, and peas. As things came in season, from our garden
she canned everything she could can, and we ate what she couldn't.
We bought, or sometimes had given to us, "drops" (fruit that had fall-
en) from orchards in the area. Fruit falls when it is overripe, during a
windstorm, or when worms get into it.

We picked raspberries, blackberries, strawberries, and mostly blueberries, ourselves. The kids would go off with small peanut butter or
shortening pails to pick, and bigger metal water pails to fill. If we picked
more than we could can or eat fresh, we sold them. We'd eat our fill during
the day while picking and still have room for a blueberry pie for supper.

All of this canning was done on an old kitchen wood stove in the heat of the season—six or seven jars at a time. My mother still had to cook three meals a day on that stove and heat water for baths and for doing laundry. God knows how those old people lived so long.

We had many meals of boiled apples—worms cut out—as you saved the best apples for canning. Same was done with the vegetables. The best was canned. Potatoes, turnips, carrots, cabbage, and parsnip were stored fresh in the cool basement. What we couldn't eat or can was fed to the cat or chickens.

It was often my job in the winter to go down into the basement— by an outside door—and bring up canned food and stored vegetables. When something like potatoes seemed to be going too fast, I'd tell my parents, and we'd eat fewer potatoes and more turnip for a while.

If something was starting to rot, I'd separate the good from the bad and bring the bad upstairs to the kitchen. There the rot was cut away, and anything that was salvageable was cooked as soon as possible. My favourite vegetable was peas, and my favourite jam was plum. Both were seemingly in perpetual short supply. It was always a treat to spread that wonderful plum jam on a hot-from-the-oven slice of bread.

A batch of canned vegetables could go bad. The snap lid bulging upward was the indicator. If we opened a jar and it smelled bad, we wouldn't eat the contents. If there was no "off" smell, we boiled it and ate it.

I didn't see a "canning guide," put out by the Department of Health, until I was in my thirties. But they recommended—no, *insisted*, if memory serves—that you discard anything with a bulged lid, whether it smelled bad or not. You could die of botulism. We survived, and so did the chickens and cats to which we fed the more questionable stuff. We did lose a lot of cats, but I think they ran away, seeking a menu with more meat.

We lost no chickens—but now that I think of it, they all had a sort of stumble in their walk and stared at you in a dazed kind of way. I just put it down to inbreeding at the time.

FALL FAIRS

THE KIDS ARE BACK IN SCHOOL AND WORK ON THE FARM has slowed down. The hay mows and the silos are full, and most of the crops are sold or in cold storage. Soon it will be winter. When the days get a little cooler and the flies are gone, it will be time to get the winter's wood under cover. In the winter they will work in the barns or sheds repairing farm machinery and look after the animals—all in from the pasture for the winter. Right now, though, there is a little break in mid-September.

It is a great time for a fall fair. It is first and foremost an agricultural event. The 4-H, the Young Farmers, or whatever other farm groups may be in the area, take an active part. Every decent-sized rural community used to hold one. The boards of directors were comprised of farmers—working farmers.

They held competitions for the Queen of the Fair, had live music, home-cooked meals, and exhibits of fruit, vegetables, jams and jellies, woodcrafts, blankets, sewing and other cottage products. Red and blue ribbons went to the winners. There were demonstrations of roping, barrel jumping, and a dozen other events. And a Midway!

Ah, the Midway—the Ferris wheel, the Tilt-A-Whirl, the carousels, and other rides, cotton candy, and, in those politically incorrect times: "Step right up! Three balls for a quarter. Knock down the Eskimo doll and win a teddy bear for your lady!" And in the next booth,

"Shoot the Indian, young man, and win the prize of your choice, ten cents a shot, step right up and show the people how good a shot you are, step right up, step right up!" And more cotton candy and ice cream and popcorn and a beer tent for the adults.

You saw people here that you hadn't seen all year. Young people, people living away now, old weather-beaten farmers, preachers, politicians, the rich and the poor.

How many young people found their first love here? How many older people who wouldn't go out to a dance came here and met new people, made new friends, found someone with whom to while away the lonely winter? How many farmers discussed crop yields, prices, shortage of workers, and the weather with other farmers?

School kids, whose parents would not allow them to go through the week, got to go on the weekend. Everyone went to the fair. It was really a harvest fair—a celebration of the growing season's end and a bit of frivolity before that final preparation for winter.

Then the fall fair "moved uptown" and became The Exhibition. They changed the dates to July or August to attract the tourists, and the locals stayed away in droves. Unfortunately, summer is when most farmers are busiest and can only make a half-hearted attempt at full participation. How do you judge fruit and vegetables that aren't harvested or jams and jellies when the ingredients aren't even ripe yet? How do you get volunteers to cook those hearty meals in the heat of the summer?

Most of these exhibitions are only a shadow of their former selves—a trap for tourists, a summer babysitter for bored kids, a petting zoo for children, and an excuse to have a Midway. If there's a real fall fair in your area, visit it now. Get as far away from the city as you can to the most remote little community that holds one—and walk and sit and smell and taste and listen to a fading piece of history. These fairs, like the passenger train, will soon be gone forever, existing only in our memories.

IVORY SOAP

<hr>

MY LIFELONG AFFAIR WITH IVORY SOAP BEGAN IN ART class, somewhere around grade six or seven. The teacher asked us all to bring in a bar of it, as we were going to learn the basics of sculpting. At the time we were using Sunlight soap at home—when we ran out of homemade soap. My mother made the homemade variety with lye, ashes, and fat, if memory serves. I don't remember what colour it was, but probably a suspicious grey colour. Sunlight was yellow.

Ivory is white—pure white. The label says it is 99.44% PURE, CLEAN, AND SIMPLE. I always wondered, though, what constituted the other approximately half of one per cent. Is it made up of impure, dirty, and "it's complicated"? Has anyone tested it lately to make sure their claim of 99.44% pure is valid?

So, when I brought a bar of Sunlight into class, it got a good few laughs from some of the rich kids. The teacher said nothing, as I suppose she knew that my parents weren't going to spend money on something as frivolous and wasteful as carving up the expensive soap and throwing it away. A couple of kids had no soap at all, so they got more grief from the elite than I did.

Anyway, I loved the smell of Ivory in the classroom and the purity of the colour as well, I suppose. The first time I got to buy my own soap, it was Ivory. It's been Ivory ever since. I don't use shampoo, either. I wash my hair with Ivory. (My hair started going white in my twenties, but that is simply a coincidence. My mother's did as well, and she never used Ivory.)

But that day in art class, I carved the most wonderfully imperfect seagull out of Sunlight soap. One of the rich kids pointed out to the class that it was the only yellow seagull he had ever seen. The teacher quieted him quickly with, "And I've never seen albino beavers and turtles, either."

HIGH SCHOOL SHOP CLASS

I DON'T REMEMBER ANYTHING I MADE IN WOODWORK-
ing class. I'm sure I wasn't very good at it, and anything I made quickly fell apart. I vaguely remember wooden mixing spoons, but if anyone
could make a defective one, it was me. I do recall what I made in metal-
working class, though. I made three things. I still have two of them.

The one I *don't* have was a toothbrush rack which we hung by
the mirror over the kitchen sink. (Our "bathroom" was outdoors.)
The rack would accommodate eight or ten brushes. It had an upward
curved lip at the bottom suitable for holding a tube of toothpaste. We
didn't use that feature, however, as the box of Cow Brand Baking Soda
that we were still using for cleaning teeth wouldn't fit. I'm guessing the
rack finally fell apart and was discarded after I'd left home.

The second item is a metal strongbox about nine inches long by
four inches wide by three and a half inches deep. It's fitted with a hasp
to accommodate a padlock—which I never bought. It's painted bright
red and has a decal on the top—a Dutch scene of a family, in wooden
shoes, near a windmill.

I keep papers of varied importance in it: my student activity card
from Northern Illinois University, my Nova Scotia Liquor Licence—
which you were required to have in order to buy booze, at any age, in
the 1960s, some of my high school report cards, my old, long-expired

passport, and my membership card in the Cattleman's Club in Palestine, Texas—the only place in town to get a cold beer on a hot Sunday the summer that I hitchhiked to Mexico. Someday I must buy a padlock. Who'd want to lose those treasures?

The third item, which means the most to me, is a plain metal dustpan painted a light green colour. I proudly gave this to my mother when I was about sixteen. She put it away, never used it, keeping it in pristine condition for about fifty years. She had items from her other kids as well. She kept these treasures, mostly wrapped, tucked away in boxes and trunks.

Some mothers and fathers are like that. I know I've kept every card and letter my daughter ever wrote to me. I suspect during those many years when we were living far apart my mother took out her prized possessions many times, held them, and thought about her children. She proudly gave the dustpan back to me, along with a poem I wrote, and some pictures I drew, when she was eighty-eight—about a year before she died.

I'd put it in my will to be buried with it, but someone would surely joke that the trash went in the coffin along with the dustpan.

You Know What I Miss?

I MISS THE TWO OLD MEN SITTING ON A BENCH IN FRONT of the general store. They greeted all who entered and left. One lit his pipe, the other pulled out his "makin's" and papers and rolled one. They were harmless old men, laughing and commenting on the weather, crops, politics, or the fall fair. A young child would boldly sit down with her bottle of Orange Crush, and the men quickly made room. She was no imposter. A stranger might think they were her grandfathers. They joked, made her laugh, and asked how her family was.

She got home safely, for at least one of them kept an eye out as she wandered down the road kicking stones and picking daisies for her mother. Turning into her driveway, she waved goodbye to them, the wrapped pound of bologna for supper tucked safely under her arm. Then the old men focused once again on the business at hand. A few minutes later they'd get up and lean against the wall, vacating the bench for a woman and her three kids who wanted to rest with the groceries before beginning their long walk home. She chatted with them. They offered a ride. She gratefully accepted. Times changed and the bench disappeared.

Then the old general store closed—the store where you dealt with the owner and family who appreciated your business, big or small. The chains took over, and now instead of a pleasant greeting as you enter the store, you often meet only a blank stare. The first words you are likely to hear are when they key in your purchases: "Is that all?" You say yes and they say, "That's twelve fifty-five." You won't hear please and thank you, and they sure as hell don't ask how your family is keeping.

I miss seeing a drinking fountain or two in nearly every community—a cold drink on a hot and dusty day. Where there was no fountain, you could go into any store or restaurant and they would be glad to give you that cold drink—free, of course. They would ask, "How's your family?" Then the fountains disappeared and stores started *selling* water.

I miss walking down the road and having neighbours stop what they are doing to wave. Maybe they were splitting firewood or unloading a truck or wagon, so you stopped in and gave them a hand. They thanked you and often asked you to stay for lunch or supper. Now everyone *drives* down the road, eyes straight ahead, and you may see a neighbour only at the chain store or at Christmastime—if you go to church. You can think of nothing to say when you do see them. You no longer know your neighbours.

Life goes on, though. We are just all indoors watching TV, or on our computers, playing with electronic toys, and shutting out the rest of the world. We go out for work or to shop, and we drive there, out of our neighbourhood, to a place where we know even fewer.

We don't worry about the single mother who moved in next door and is barely getting by. They have no car. They're not from here. They are "welfare people." At work by the water cooler the discussion is about why there is so much depression and other mental illness.

A few months later, we shake our heads in dismay and wonder why her son would walk into the woods that day and take his own life. We discuss all the details of the story with complete strangers at work, but we haven't visited his mother yet, because we don't know her.

She'll move away. The images of the yellow police tape, the cops and the coroner walking silently out of the woods carrying his body on a stretcher, his mother all but collapsing as she fights to stop reality—they will all slowly fade, and we'll forget her and her nightmare. When the next family moves in, we won't visit them—until we "get to know them better." We need to find out what "kind" they are, first.

I think there was less suffering and hunger and loneliness when we all knew each other. I believe we had more fun when all were included.

Today we know much more about the famous, the celebrated, and wars in far-off lands than we do about those who live like us and near us. And in all of our enlightenment about the larger world, we have become ignorant of, and deaf and blind to, the needs of those around us. Surely we are all the poorer for it.

My First Apartment

IT WAS JUST OFF QUEEN STREET IN HALIFAX, AND MY FIRST place wasn't really a full apartment. I guess that's why it was advertised as APART FOR RENT. It had a bedroom—of sorts. This was an area off the main part of the unfinished basement, separated from the furnace and the rest of the open basement by a curtain. It was wintertime, and when in bed, your front, facing the furnace was hot, while your backside froze. You had to keep turning around in bed to try to even up the temperature.

The old oil furnace would cut in with a snap and a bang about every hour. I'd wake up then and turn over. It was the only time in my life when I was hot and cold simultaneously. There was that brief ten-minute period, though, after you turned over, as your hot parts cooled and your cool parts warmed, that your body achieved uniformity of temperature. I learned to fall back asleep in that "sweet spot."

I had no kitchen, not even a hot plate. My "bedroom" had a single bed and a stool—that's all, folks. I kept my alarm clock and ashtray on the stool. There was a bathroom, which was comprised of a big laundry tub that doubled as a sink next to the washer and dryer, a rusty shower stall with no curtain, and an ancient china fixture that had to be a clone of the one John Crapper patented as the world's first flush toilet.

All of this was out in the open of a concrete basement. The land-lady was often down there doing laundry for her "boarders," all of whom lived upstairs. How I envied those guys. If I was "in the bathroom," I was to start singing or whistling when the basement door opened, and then the landlady would turn back and wait for a while. The only places to sit in my apartment were on the toilet or on the bed.

There was a basement window—with no curtain—and if you looked up and out of it, you could see the ankles of passersby. In that cobwebbed window was an old radio—set up high there so you could get some reception other than static. I'd listen to it late at night, "on the skip," when stations in the US would come in quite strongly. As one station faded, I'd have to get up out of bed and work the dial to find another. As you might suspect, I listened to a lot of blues on those late winter nights.

It was the only apartment I ever had with no key. The back door of the house was left unlocked—day and night—and the stairs leading down to the basement were right there in the back porch. The landlady was always home, anyway.

I had absolutely no company the whole time I was there. How could you invite a woman into a place like that? I went there only late at night to sleep. I'd read and write, sitting on the bed, and I emptied numerous bottles of Schooner beer.

I'd dream of a "better place" to live, and within months I had enough money to get one. It wasn't *much* better, but it was an improvement—with a proper toilet, walls, doors, and a hot plate.

The worst part in the old place was the loneliness—especially on a stormy Sunday when I was off work but couldn't go out. Those were long days. It might have been the beer, but I found that if I ran around my tiny cot at just the right speed, I could almost meet myself going down the other side.

That's the closest I came to company. Being alone helps you get to know yourself better, but when you are as warped as me, that's not good for your mental health.

Scadding House

IN WATCHING RECENT TV DOCUMENTARIES ON THE '60s and '70s, a flood of old memories rolled in: Marching and protesting the Vietnam War in downtown Toronto. Hanging around on the weekends in Yorkville, with the generation that was going to change the world. And sitting with American draft dodgers, runaways, street kids, and hippies at Scadding House at Trinity Square, downtown.

Scadding House was a drop-in centre situated next to the Church of the Holy Trinity. It had been the rectory of Rev. Henry Scadding. A mansion in its time, it still had its open staircase to the second floor. Now it was a place to hang out, play board games and Ping-Pong, read, and have a free cup of coffee. My brother, who lived in the city volunteered there. I was living and working out on the Niagara Peninsula, and sometimes on the weekends I'd come in to visit him and hang out while he was working.

They allowed no booze or drugs, and it was an amazingly peaceful place. Right next to the church, it seemed almost a part of it. I think that may have kept the rowdy crowd away. Some of the guys and girls toked grass, and most smoked cigarettes. They went outside to do it in a most mannerly way. I met a lot of kids from all over the country and a few Americans. A number of connections were made between people who had no one else to turn to and nowhere else to go. Several romances bloomed. I learned a bit about the blues.

I was following folk singers—Dylan, Lightfoot, Pete Seeger, and others—at the time. What I knew about black music was the doo-wop groups and Motown.

The real Delta Blues was a new experience for me. I met a local guy there, a white guy—Rick—who was totally into the blues, and he had stacks of record albums and old 78s of everything.

I went to see him and the group he performed with at Grossman's Tavern, out on Spadina, and thoroughly enjoyed it—although they did not stick to just the raw blues. I still have one of their albums. But along with the music, I remember what he used to do at Scadding to amuse us—particularly those who'd had a few tokes. He was a big, heavy guy and could make the floor shake when he walked around.

He'd sit about halfway up the stairs to the second floor, and slowly slide, as if by accident, down onto the next step with a big thump. Then he'd look sideways at us with a surprised expression. He'd repeat this, gaining speed until he reached the bottom step. We'd all clap. You had to be there, as they say, but it was funny as hell—especially to those who had a buzz going. It's a wonder he didn't damage his spine.

Once in a while I'll hear "Flip Flop Fly" by the Downchild Blues Band with Rick, his brother Don—the leader—and the others, and the strongest visual I have of Downchild is Rick sliding down those stairs at Scadding House. You don't have to be sad all the time to sing the blues. RIP—Rick Walsh.

The Fight with Peter

WHEN I WAS ABOUT AGE TWENTY-TWO, A DISAGREE-
ment with my best friend, Peter, almost came to blows. He believes it did. Peter was drunk that night and came by my place with his
girlfriend. I was stone cold sober. They were going to a club, and he wanted me to come along with them. I declined, but he would not take no for
an answer. He wanted to fight me. The winner would decide whether we
all went to the club or stayed for the evening at my apartment.

Stupid, eh? But that's how young guys can be when they're drunk.

I told him I wouldn't fight him, and his girlfriend tried to talk him
out of it, but he was bound and determined. We were outside when
he started swinging at me. I bobbed and weaved and circled, and he
couldn't touch me. My hands hardly left my sides. Getting frustrated
and perhaps a little dizzy from all the alcohol, he swung with a big
haymaker, missed, and fell to the ground. He hit my knee as he went
down. He knocked himself out, or passed out. Patti and I brought him
around and finally got him to his feet.

"What in the hell did you hit me with, Pike?" he slurred.

"Nothing," I told him, but he wouldn't believe me.

We got him into the house, got some coffee in him, and his girlfriend applied ice to the black eye he gave himself when he hit my
knee. The next day, he refused to believe that he simply fell, that I

hadn't touched him. He wasn't angry. He accepted that he had started the fight. He was amazed, though, at how good a fighter I was!

Peter was not a fighter, although I saw him break up a few brawls. He wasn't a guy to tangle with. Next time we were in the tavern, we ran into a couple buddies. They asked about the black eye.

Peter said to the boys, "You're looking at the guy, right there, who did this to me. Laurie kicked my ass. I wouldn't have believed it. I couldn't lay a glove on him. He went up one side of me and down the other. Then he kicked me with both boots—at the same time! I couldn't believe it when I saw two feet coming at me. Then he hit me with something, maybe a baseball bat, I don't know, and down I went. Stay away from this guy. He's just too good."

I just laughed it off, but it gave me a bit of street cred with the other guys.

Peter died some thirty years ago, but as long as he lived, he believed that I had whipped him. Neither Patti nor I could convince him otherwise. Had he been sober, I would have defended myself, but I still would not have hit him. I gave up fighting when I was in junior high. Had he been sober, of course, he would not have started a fight.

I loved Peter like a brother. We were closer than any of the brothers I had. I wish he knew that I did not hit him. Maybe he did know but just thought his version was a good narrative. Peter loved telling stories. But he always warned the guys we met not to pick a fight with me.

"Leave him alone," he'd tell them, "you won't even see it coming!"

My First Real Estate Deal

THEY WERE LIKE A SECOND FAMILY, ALTHOUGH I WAS only a boarder (their sons jokingly called me the Nova Scotia Boarder or the Malicious Roomer). I was treated as one of the family. When Jack and Lil Connell decided one summer to take the family back home to Nova Scotia for vacation, I stayed behind.

I was working full-time on night crew in a supermarket and already had my vacation planned for a hitchhike to Mexico later in the summer. Lil was uneasy about leaving me there alone. "What will you eat? Will you be okay? Are you sure you don't mind?" I didn't mind, as with a very quiet house during their absence it would be much easier to get to sleep in the mornings after work.

"Don't worry about me," I told her. "If I were you, I'd be worrying about leaving my house and all my worldly possessions with a penniless young single guy." We all laughed, but I knew I had to come up with a prank to scare them when they returned.

Lil cooked up several casseroles and put them in the freezer for me. The next morning, I waved goodbye to them, as Jack and Lil and their three sons drove away for a two-week holiday. Before going to bed, I took a sledgehammer out of the trunk, drove a metal frame into the front lawn, and hung a real estate FOR SALE sign on it.

Next door, I saw the curtain close just as I looked toward it. Betty lived here, and she knew everything that happened on the street, who was doing what to whom, and whether it was dead of night or middle of the day, she kept her watch. The young people on Bunnell Drive called her the "President of the Burlington Binocular Club," with good reason.

If a young lady wanted to kiss her date good night, she'd do it up around the corner, or tomorrow Betty would have them "making love in the back seat, right across from my house, don't you know!" I was glad that Betty saw me, as it was a way to get even with her. (After all, the only reason we had been in the back seat was to search for the young lady's house key, which must have fallen out of her purse when she put it back there.)

I had a coffee before I closed all the curtains and went to bed that morning. I truly expected the police to show up. The cops didn't come. Perhaps Betty wanted to see a SOLD sign first, as I would likely go to jail longer for *selling* what wasn't mine as opposed to *trying* to sell it.

The two weeks went fast, and soon it was the day before the Connells were due back. That day, I took the SOLD sticker (which I had borrowed along with the real estate sign and holder), out of the trunk of my car and applied it diagonally across the FOR SALE. I turned quickly and saw Betty's curtains fall back together.

The cops did come that morning, and I handed them the business card of the real estate agent. "Call him," I told them, "and he will tell you that we are simply playing a prank on our mutual friends." They did, he did, and all was well.

We had a great laugh when the Connells returned. I remember Jack telling the story to guests at our numerous parties over the next few years. Whenever there was someone new there, someone I hadn't met before, Jack would say, "Years ago we had a boarder, and one summer we went on vacation and left him here alone.

"I told Lil, 'You're going to regret this,' but that woman wouldn't listen. I warned her. I knew what he was like. I figured he might sell the silverware or her good china, but I didn't care—we never use that stuff anyway. But we got some shock when we returned.

"We saw the real estate sign from a distance, but it looked like it was on Betty's lawn. But as we got closer, Lil looked at me with eyes as big as saucers. 'My God! We've been sold, Jack! We've been sold!'" Then Jack would introduce me to the new people as the Nova Scotia Boarder.

Betty never spoke of the matter, although I'm sure she knew that I knew who called the police. Also, I had a duplicate key made for the young lady, so we never had to scramble trying to find it in the back seat ever again.

THE GIRL FROM EEL RIVER CROSSING

I SAW HER COME UP THE STEPS, AND I COULDN'T LOOK away. Some experiences are so fleeting that you forget them. It may be a simple smile, a touch on the arm, or an unexpected act of kindness. Others are over quickly as well but are so powerful that you will remember them forever. This is an event that, while blurry around the edges, is one which I have never forgotten.

I met the pretty lady on a train from New Brunswick to Montreal in the 1960s. I was going on to Toronto, back to work from a vacation in Nova Scotia. Later, she told me that she was on her way to visit some family in Montreal. I sensed, somehow, that this was a cover story as she didn't know me well enough to get into the details. She'd come down by car from Eel River Crossing, New Brunswick, a small francophone community up near Campbellton, and boarded the *Ocean Limited* at Grand Falls.

I was in my early twenties. I guessed her to be about twenty. She took the row of seats opposite me in the almost empty passenger coach. Her hair was coal black, her pretty face café au lait, she was French but either had some Aboriginal blood or was very well tanned. I had trouble taking my eyes off her, but she just smiled when she caught me, showing more pearly white teeth than anyone has a right to own. She took some comic books out of a travel bag.

The child with her was not old enough to read and barely old enough to read to. She began reading a French-language comic book out loud and showing him the pictures. When the boy fell asleep, we started chatting.

A single mother, she said, and she spoke English with a very attractive French accent. I asked if I could read one of her comics. She passed me a couple, but I don't remember now what they were. When I came to words that I didn't understand and I looked puzzled, she'd lean across the aisle and whisper the translation to me. I also asked her some words and phrases that I *did* know just to hear her soft, musical voice.

With the child now sleeping soundly in the window seat on her side, she moved away from me into the middle seat and beckoned me to move across—to the aisle seat that she had just vacated. "Come over, Lo-ray. Me? I will read it in the Anglais to you."

We leaned back in the seats, and she began reading, more in a whisper now, as it was late and some of the passengers were sleeping. I was almost hypnotized by her voice, her perfume. Mesmerized by the closeness of this beautiful woman. We read for a while and then continued to talk in whispers, for hours—half the night.

We laughed, joked, and talked about our lives, each practising our second language on the other. She was unclear about how long she would be in Montreal and why she was going. I didn't want to pry. I think we both fell asleep at about the same time.

The porter must have turned off our light. When I awoke later, she was cuddled into me in the darkness, her head on my chest and her hand holding mine.

I don't know if she was dreaming that I was someone else, or if she wanted to be close to me. When I'd move a little, however, she'd move closer and grip my hand tighter. I didn't mind. I stayed awake for a long time, listening to the hypnotic song that the rails were singing. She and her boy slept soundly. Somewhere, west of Quebec City, as the *Ocean Limited* rocked and rolled its way through the night, I fell in love with her.

I don't remember waking up in the morning, but I do remember getting off at Montreal. I had to catch another train for Toronto, with very little time to spare. We went in opposite directions. I looked back, but she had disappeared into the crowd. I assume someone met her and her child.

I also remember, while still on the train, giving her my mailing address, and her promising to write to me *ce soir*, when she got to her destination. I didn't take her address, as she didn't know how long she would be in Montreal. She would update me and tell me where to send my reply when she wrote.

I promised I would come to see her when she got back to New Brunswick. I recall us kissing long and passionately, just before we left the train. She did not want to break the embrace. We held each other for a long time. I remember tears. Then she was gone, and I was on the *Canadian* to Toronto, alone but still feeling that too-rare warm glow.

Fate. I was struck by the thought that we had somehow met for a reason—that this was not just a chance meeting—that this was the start of something special for both of us.

That's not exactly how the story ends, though. When I got back to Burlington, where I lived, I told my "second family" about her and asked Lil, my "second mother," to watch for a letter. Each day for a few weeks I asked about it. I wanted this woman, and I couldn't understand why she hadn't written. Slowly, I came to realize that she wasn't going to write.

Maybe she had a husband and our "tryst" had just been a fling for her. Perhaps she was only lonely that night. Could she have met someone else?

I met another woman, and *la belle dame* faded from my daily thoughts. Eventually I even forgot her name.

Some years later, after I had married and subsequently divorced, I was visiting my second family, the Connells, and sitting with Lil at the kitchen table having a beer. I reminded her about the girl that I had met on the train and, while I couldn't remember her name, wondered out loud if she had been the girl for me.

I told Lil that I couldn't believe that she hadn't written. I was so certain that she would. Lil's response came as a shock.

"Don't hold it against her, Laurie. She wrote to you. I didn't tell you because I thought she was wrong for you—you know, with a child and all. I didn't want you to get hurt."

"What? Do you still have the letter?"

"No, Laurie, I'm sorry. I didn't read it or anything. I just burned it in the fireplace."

I was angry. How could she? As stunning as this revelation was, I couldn't stay angry with Lil. I'm sure she wished she hadn't done it, and she would never do it again.

At the time, though, she thought of me as her own son and just wanted to protect me from making what she believed would be a bad mistake.

What had the young lady told me in that letter? Did she have feelings for me, too? Did she later wonder why I didn't write back? Would she never know how hard I fell for her?

Eel River Crossing is a very small community in northern New Brunswick. The next time that I got down east by car, I made a detour and went up to have a look around. There wasn't much to see—a few dozen houses spread along a narrow winding road.

I went into a little dépanneur/general store, bought a Coke, and asked could I look at their phone book. I searched up and down through the surnames to see if any name would jump off the page. None did. It had been too long.

But I've never forgotten the night she clung to me like she needed somebody to hold her. Who knows what she had to do in Montreal? Maybe she was giving up her son for adoption. Perhaps she would end up dancing in a bar to feed her child.

I'll always remember her whispering in two languages and the fragrance of her raven hair. Remember her warm brown eyes and the taste of her lips. Remember her hand gestures when she explained in French what Moose is going to do to Reggie for flirting with Midge. Yeah! I remember now—one of those comic books was an Archie, sure!

So—maybe someday I'll also remember her name. Years ago, I used to think that if I ever did, I'd find out where she lives. I'd write her a letter—just to let her know why she never heard from me.

Later, I decided against trying to find her. Ships do pass in the night. She is no doubt a grandmother or a great-grandmother by now. Who knows what her life has been like? It would serve no good purpose to remind her of a long-forgotten missed connection.

So, I didn't and won't try to reach her. It would be nice, though, if she knew that I didn't just blow her off—that I would have done anything to be with her. That I will always remember the young lady whom I sensed was headed somewhere that she really didn't want to go. That I wish I could have helped—wish I could have done more for her, because I think she needed me—so long ago.

THE MEANING OF NFG

A S I WAS MAKING THE TRANSITION FROM THE RETAIL grocery business to outside sales in my twenties, I took a job with an appliance manufacturer. I was only there a short time. They had insisted that I work for a few weeks in the factory before going out on the road selling for them. They wanted all their sales force to thoroughly understand how a fridge or a washing machine was put together.

My first job was applying the insulation to the walls of the refrigerators. They hadn't told me I should wear a long-sleeved shirt instead of a T-shirt like the others on the assembly line. After the first shift, I was sweaty in that old building with little ventilation and no air conditioning. Then I got itchy.

Having a beer with a couple of co-workers afterwards, they explained that the fibreglass was getting into the pores of my arms. The trick was to wash afterwards with cold water and wipe the arms off in a downward motion. Most of the fibres would come out. Next day, as suggested, I wore a long-sleeved shirt.

I was on a different job the next day, however, and sweated in the same shirt. That job function was feeding the line with parts. The following day I wore a T-shirt, and my job was spot welding—with sparks flying around. They suggested that I put on my jacket to protect my arms.

I sweated again. Clearly there was little communication between the sales department and factory, as this training was not being conducted in any orderly way.

When I'd get ahead of the rest of the line, the foreman would tell me to go take a break. When I'd come back, all hands were sitting down waiting for the missing guy (me) to catch up again. With other workers going to the washroom, the line stopped and started all day.

The people were all super, but the foreman and the shop steward would not let the workers do a day's work. Small wonder that the industry was moving more of its manufacturing offshore. Highly paid union jobs frittered away—sent to places where people wanted to work. Soon I simply lost respect for the management and left for another job.

But while I was there, I worked on the line with one older lady named Joan who had a great sense of humour. She was a small, shrivelled-up old woman, and she had a hunched back. They had a joke going where any new worker was told to ask her about the weather. They claimed her predictions were amazing. They got me on my first day.

"Do you think it will rain tomorrow, Joan?"

"I don't know, but I sure have a hunch," she replied with a straight face. You'd never mention the weather to her again, and they wouldn't tell you she was in on the joke, until days later.

My last day there, I was working with her on inspections at the end of the line. From there the appliances were loaded on skids and sent to inventory. I noticed some fridges off to the side with words scribbled in grease pencil. The notes indicated the deficiency so that unit could be repaired.

That afternoon she marked a couple units NW, which she said meant that they are not working when you plugged them in. Later in the day she marked some NFG.

"What does that mean?" I asked her.

"That means that there are too many things wrong with it and it will have to be stripped down and rebuilt," she told me. I should have known better, but I had to ask.

"But what do the initials NFG stand for?"

"No f*****g good!" the lady told me—and she did not speak in asterisks.

At least I left the job on my last day with a smile.

Laurie Blackwood Pike, a.k.a. Grandpa Pike, was born in Stanhope, Newfoundland and Labrador. He is retired from his position as business development manager with a national chain of hardware and building supply stores. In 2017, he received the Estwing Gold Hammer Award—the industry's recognition for his contributions. In 1986, he bought a rural general store, developed a logo, and branded the business "Grandpa Pike's." His unique store was profiled in the hardware industry's *Hardware Merchandising* magazine. In recent years, Grandpa Pike has used his nickname for charity work. In 2007, he partnered with the Children's Wish Foundation of Canada, Newfoundland & Labrador Chapter, to release a music CD. In 2009, he partnered with them again to produce a gospel Christmas CD. He is married to Kathleen Pike and has one daughter, Laurie Shannon. *Grandpa Pike's Number Two* is his third book. His second, *A Man of My Word*, is the critically acclaimed biography of former premier Beaton Tulk. His first book, *Grandpa Pike's Outhouse Reader*, has appeared in *Atlantic Books Today*'s bestsellers lists.